Sunset

Brilliant
Kitchens

By the Editors of Sunset Books and Sunset Magazine

*An overhead pot rack provides both focus and function. For a
closer look at this kitchen, see pages 28–29.*

Sunset Publishing Corporation ▪ **Menlo Park, California**

Custom touches make a difference. Here, a range-side niche provides a spot for display shelves and decorative prints. Architect: Kirby Fitzpatrick.

Book Editor
Scott Atkinson

Coordinating Editor
Suzanne Normand Mathison

Design
Joe di Chiarro

Illustrations
Mark Pechenik

Photographers: **ARX Photography,** 84 left; **Richard Barnes,** 6; **Glenn Christiansen,** 71 middle; **Christina del Villar,** 70 top, 82; **Philip Harvey,** 5 top, 50, 87 left; **Grant Huntington,** 4; **Leonard Lammi,** 83 top; **David Livingston,** 80 left; **Stephen Marley,** 60; **Miele Appliances, Inc.,** 79 top, 80 right; **Norman A. Plate,** 71 top; **Kenneth Rice,** 52 bottom, 53; **Showcase Kitchens,** 40 bottom; **Smallbone, Inc.,** 22; **JoAnn Masaoka Van Atta,** 65 left; **John Vaughan,** 30 left, 52 top, 76; **Alan Weintraub,** 58, 59; **Russ Widstrand,** 5 bottom right, 38, 39, 40 top, 41, 62 top left, 69 middle left and bottom left, 71 bottom, 81, 91 bottom, 92; **Tom Wyatt,** 1, 2, 5 bottom left, 21, 24, 25, 26, 27, 28, 29, 30 right, 31, 32, 33, 34, 35, 36, 37, 42, 43, 44, 45, 46, 47, 48, 49, 51, 54, 55, 56, 57, 62 top right and bottom, 65 right, 68, 69 top left, top right, and bottom right, 70 middle and bottom, 72, 73, 74, 75, 77, 78, 79 middle and bottom, 83 middle left and right, 84 right, 85, 86, 87 right, 88, 89, 90, 91 top left and right.

In Pursuit of the Perfect Kitchen . . .

Plot the kitchen of your dreams with this new *Sunset* title as your guide. You'll find the latest in both gleaming cooktops and efficient designs. From a cozy armchair, you can examine case studies—18 up-to-the-minute kitchen designs in full-color. Or bone up on European cabinets, convection ovens, commercial ranges, and halogen downlights. If you're ready to dig in, you'll also find a solid introduction to kitchen planning, as practiced by the pros.

Many kitchen professionals and homeowners provided information and encouragement or let us take a look at their new creations. We'd especially like to thank the National Kitchen & Bath Association, Hackettstown, New Jersey; and Nicholas J. Geragi, Jr., of The Room Designer™, East Syracuse, New York. We'd also like to acknowledge Allmilmö Showplace; Bath & Beyond; BK Design Studio; Custom Countertops; Miele Appliances, Inc.; Gene Schick & Co.; Hollis Shaw; and the Northern California Kitchen & Bath Association.

Special thanks go to Rene Lynch for carefully editing the manuscript, to JoAnn Masaoka Van Atta for scouting locations and styling many of the photos, and to Lynne B. Tremble and Barbara Widstrand for photo help in Southern California.

Cover: Graceful curves of cabinets, island, and ceiling soffit lead the eye into this inviting white kitchen. Architect: J. Allen Sayles/Architectural Kitchens & Baths. Cover design by Susan Bryant. Photography by Philip Harvey. Photo styling by JoAnn Masaoka Van Atta.

Editor, Sunset Books: Elizabeth L. Hogan

First printing May 1991

Brilliant Kitchens Copyright © 1991 Sunset Publishing Corporation, Menlo Park, CA 94025. First edition. Library of Congress Catalog Card Number: 91-65560. ISBN 0-376-01234-X.

The contents of this book are also published in Sunset *Ideas for Great Kitchens* and as part of Sunset *Kitchen Remodeling Handbook.*

Kitchen Remodeling Handbook Copyright © 1983, 1976, 1974, 1967, 1962, 1955, Sunset Publishing Coorporation, Menlo Park, CA 94025. Library of Congress Catalog Card Number: 83-81005. ISBN 0-376-01345-1.

Ideas for Great Kitchens Copyright © 1991, Sunset Publishing Corporation, Menlo Park, CA 94025. Library of Congress Catalog Card Number: 90-71270. ISBN 0-376-01236-6.

CONTENTS

WHAT'S COOKING?

Super-efficient, flexible, and a little bit of fun—that's the recipe for the contemporary kitchen. More varied than ever, kitchen design features sparkling new colors, fresh styles, and varied components.

Many homeowners appreciate the clean lines and bright colors of the European-style kitchen. Its frameless cabinets, in high-gloss lacquer or laminate, hide efficient aids such as lazy Susans and wire-frame pullouts. Appliances are built in, from refrigerator and microwave oven to the toaster. Even sinks and faucets come in new shapes and colors.

On the other hand, cheery country and traditional styles remain popular. Often the focus of a kitchen is its freestanding range, especially

DESIGNER: SUSAN BRITTON

one of the high-output "residential/ commercial" models. Adding warmth and hospitality are homey accents like potracks, freestanding furniture, open shelving or display soffits, custom backsplashes, and oak flooring.

Open kitchens give a feeling of spaciousness; many accommodate personal options like two-cook layouts, baking centers, or areas for informal entertaining. Popular as ever are kitchen islands and peninsulas, which define the work area yet allow the cook to converse freely with family and friends.

Planning a new kitchen is a threefold process: planning the space, defining a style, and choosing components. You can follow these steps in order or browse freely, using the book as an information source or as a collection of specific ideas to show your architect or designer.

Black European-style cabinets (facing page), granite countertops, rubber flooring, and stylish lighting represent one pole of kitchen design; a traditional "white-and-flowers" great room (below) shows the other. The colorful pullout faucet (bottom left) and modular island cooktop (bottom right) are two of many new components available.

DESIGNER: THOMAS BARTLETT INTERIORS OF NAPA

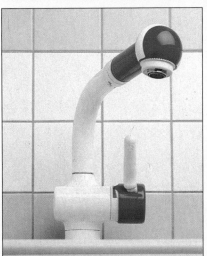

DESIGNER: KITCHENS BY STEWART

A PLANNING PRIMER

Sit back, close your eyes, and visualize your dream kitchen. Do images of shiny new cabinets and appliances float before your eyes? Now come down to earth. What's the clearance between the dishwasher and the new island? If you're stumped trying to fit the pieces together, you're not alone.

Use this chapter as a *workbook*, a sequential course in basic kitchen planning. Begin by evaluating your existing kitchen; wind your way through layout and design basics; then finish up with a look at the professionals who can give you a hand.

For ideas and inspiration, peruse the color photos in the next two chapters, examining the case studies of existing kitchens and getting familiar with the latest in islands, downlights, and wall ovens.

The end result? That dream kitchen will reappear, this time on solid ground.

A granite-topped, five-sided island occupies the center of this kitchen, which is separated from existing living space by partial walls of exposed concrete and open-stud framing. Blue cabinet stain and red wall plaster form primary accents to gray and wood tones. Architect: Mark Mack.

TAKING STOCK

First things first: Before the fun of jumping into a kitchen shopping spree, take the time to survey what you have *now*. A clear, accurate base map—such as the one shown below—is your best planning tool. It also helps you communicate with both design professionals and showroom personnel.

Measure the space. To make your kitchen survey, you'll need either a folding wooden rule or steel measuring tape. The folding rule (shown at right) is the pro's choice: it stays rigid when extended and is good for "inside" measurements.

First, sketch out your present layout (don't worry about scale), doodling in windows, doors, islands, and other features. Then measure each wall at counter height. Here's an example, using a hypothetical kitchen: beginning at one corner, measure the distance to the outer edge of the window frame, from there to the opposite edge of the window frame, from this edge to the cabinet, and from one end of the cabinet to the corner. After you finish measuring one wall, total the figures; then take an overall measurement from corner to corner. The two figures should match. Measure the height of each wall in the same manner.

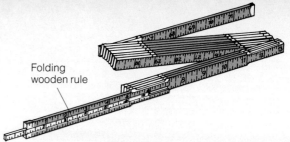

Folding wooden rule

Do the opposite walls agree? If not, something's out of level or out of plumb; find out what it is. Also check all corners with a carpenter's square or by the 3-4-5 method: measure 3 feet out from the corner in one direction, 4 feet in the other direction, and connect the points with a straightedge. If the distance is 5 feet, the corner is square.

Make a base map. Now draw your kitchen to scale on graph paper—most kitchen designers use ½-inch scale (1/24th actual size). An architect's scale is helpful but isn't really required. Some good drafting paper with ¼-inch squares and a T-square and triangle greatly simplify matters.

The example shown below includes both centerlines to the sink plumbing and electrical symbols—outlets, switches, and fixtures. It's also helpful to note the direction of joists (see page 18), mark any bearing walls, and sketch in other features that might affect your remodeling plans.

A Sample Base Map

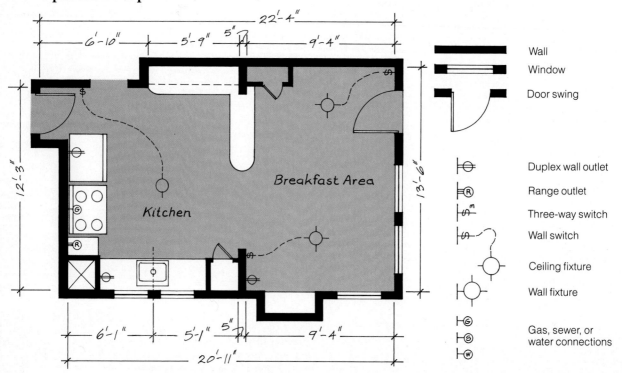

A KITCHEN QUESTIONNAIRE

A questionnaire such as the one below can help stimulate and organize your responses to your present kitchen. When used with your base map, it also provides a good starting point for discussing your ideas with architects, designers, or kitchen showroom personnel. Note your answer to each question on a separate sheet of paper, adding any important preferences or dislikes that occur. Then gather your notes, any clippings you've collected, and a copy of your base map, and you're ready to begin.

1. What's your main reason for changing your kitchen?

2. How many are in your household? List adults, teens, children, pets.

3. Are you right-handed? Left-handed? How tall?

4. Will this be a two-cook kitchen?

5. Do you entertain frequently? Formally? Informally? Do you like great-room (open) designs?

6. What secondary activity areas do you want? ☐ Baking center ☐ Planning desk ☐ Breakfast nook ☐ Laundry and ironing center ☐ Wet bar ☐ Other

7. Would you like an island or peninsula?

8. Can existing plumbing be moved? To where?

9. Is the kitchen located on the first or second floor? Is there a full basement, crawl space, or concrete slab below? Is there a second floor, attic, or open ceiling above?

10. If necessary, can present doors and windows be moved?

11. Do you want an open or vaulted ceiling?

12. What's the rating of your electrical service?

13. What type of heating system do you have?

14. Is the kitchen to be designed for a disabled person? Is the individual confined to a wheelchair?

15. What style is your home's exterior?

16. What style would you like for your kitchen? (For example, high-tech, country contemporary, country French.) Do you favor compartmentalized European layouts or a more open, informal look?

17. What color schemes do you prefer?

18. List new cabinet material to be used: wood, laminate, or other? If wood, should it be painted or stained? Light or dark? If natural, do you want oak, maple, pine, cherry?

19. Cabinet requirements: ☐ Appliance garage ☐ Pullout shelves ☐ Lazy Susan ☐ Tilt-down sink front ☐ Pantry pack ☐ Storage wall with pullout bins ☐ Tray divider ☐ Spice storage ☐ Breadbox/flatware drawer ☐ Wall oven cabinet ☐ Built-in microwave ☐ Vent hood ☐ Built-in refrigerator ☐ Utility cabinet ☐ Cutting board ☐ Knife storage ☐ Wine rack ☐ Waste basket ☐ Glass doors ☐ Open shelving ☐ Other

20. Should soffit space above cabinets be boxed in? Open for decorative articles? Cabinets continuous to ceiling?

21. What countertop materials do you prefer: ☐ Laminate ☐ Ceramic tile ☐ Solid-surface ☐ Butcher-block ☐ Stone ☐ Stainless steel? Do you want a 4" or full backsplash? More than one material?

22. List your present appliances. What new appliances are you planning? What finish: white, black, matching panel?

23. Would you prefer a vent hood or downdraft system? Do you want a decorative ceiling fan?

24. What flooring do you have? Do you need new flooring? ☐ Wood ☐ Vinyl ☐ Ceramic tile ☐ Stone ☐ Other

25. What are present wall and ceiling coverings? What wall treatments do you like? ☐ Paint ☐ Wallpaper ☐ Wood ☐ Faux finish ☐ Plaster ☐ Glass block

26. Lighting type desired: ☐ Incandescent ☐ Fluorescent ☐ Halogen ☐ 120-volt or low-voltage? What fixture types? ☐ Recessed downlights ☐ Track lights ☐ Pendant fixtures ☐ Undercabinet strips ☐ Indirect soffit lighting

27. Consider any other structural additions: ☐ Skylights ☐ Greenhouse window or sunroom ☐ Cooking alcove ☐ Passthrough ☐ Other

28. What time framework do you have for completion?

29. What budget figure do you have in mind?

BASIC KITCHEN LAYOUTS

Now the fun begins: it's time to start planning your new kitchen. While brainstorming, it helps to have some basic layout schemes in mind. The floor plans shown below have become classics—practical both for utilizing space and for incorporating an efficient work triangle (see facing page).

One-wall kitchen. Small or open kitchens frequently make use of the one-wall design, incorporating a single line of cabinets and appliances. This is not ideal, as there is a lot of moving back and forth—from refrigerator to range to sink. Still, it's the only choice for some small areas or open floor plans.

An island or peninsula (see facing page) with sink and eating area can provide needed counter space while effectively blocking out foot traffic.

Corridor kitchen. A kitchen open at both ends is a candidate for the corridor or galley kitchen; the design works well as long as the distance between opposite walls is not too great. Traffic flow can be a problem—it's tough to divert kitchen cruisers away from the cook.

L-shaped kitchen. This classic layout utilizes two adjacent walls, spreading the work centers out; typically, the refrigerator is at one end, range or wall ovens are at the other end, and the sink is in the center. The L-shaped kitchen allows a comfortable work triangle; however, now you'll have to decide how to utilize the corner space (see page 15).

U-shaped kitchen. Three adjacent walls make up the efficient U-shaped design (efficient, that is, as long as there is sufficient distance between opposite walls). Often this layout opens up space for auxiliary work areas in addition to the central work triangle—options such as a baking center, a second cooktop and dishwasher, or a complete work center for a second cook.

Great room. A *great room* is simply any large space that houses the kitchen, dining room, and living areas, thus opening up the kitchen as an entertainment space and bringing family and friends together during meal preparation time.

There are potential drawbacks. The kitchen is on constant view and work areas must be blocked out very carefully. Noise can be a problem to consider

Sample Layouts & Work Triangles

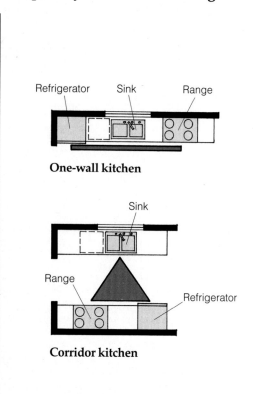

One-wall kitchen

Corridor kitchen

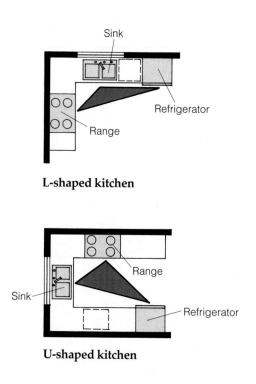

L-shaped kitchen

U-shaped kitchen

in great-room design, and privacy is obviously reduced. In remodeling, a great-room layout almost always means knocking out an existing wall or two.

Island. A kitchen island is a popular addition to many kitchen remodels: the extra cabinets and countertop add storage and work space, block off unwanted traffic flow, and can save a cook a number of steps in a large, underutilized space.

On the minus side, islands can cramp space and cut into work triangles and traffic flows. See page 15 for minimum clearance and other guidelines for sizing and placing these units.

Peninsula. A landlocked version of the island, the kitchen peninsula is an effective addition to any basic layout, assuming that there's sufficient room for traffic to move around the end. A well-planned peninsula can augment the work triangle, create a breakfast nook, break up unwanted traffic flow, and corral many storables.

It's sometimes easier to route utilities to a peninsula than to the free-floating island: gas lines, wiring, and plumbing simply come through the adjacent base or wall cabinets.

CONSIDER THE WORK TRIANGLE

Ever since kitchen layout studies in the 1950s introduced the term, designers have been evaluating kitchen efficiency by means of the *work triangle.* The three legs of the triangle connect the refrigerator, sink, and range (or cooktop). An efficient work triangle greatly reduces the steps a cook must take during meal preparation; the ideal sum of the three legs is between 12 and 23 feet. Whenever possible, the work triangle should not be interrupted by the traffic flow.

Today, the reign of the work triangle is being challenged by two-cook layouts, elaborate island work centers, peninsulas, and specialized appliances such as modular cooktops, built-in grills, and microwave and convection ovens.

New studies are under way to bring kitchen theory current with the latest designs. Nevertheless, the work triangle is still a valuable starting point for planning kitchen efficiency. One hint: Sometimes it's useful to sketch in multiple triangles to cover different requirements. If you follow the countertop guidelines discussed on pages 12–13, your basic triangle, or triangles, should fall into place.

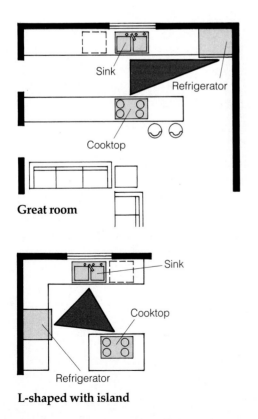

Great room

L-shaped with island

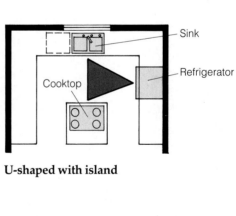

U-shaped with island

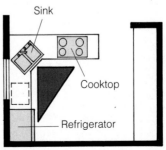

Peninsula

Kitchen Planning at a Glance

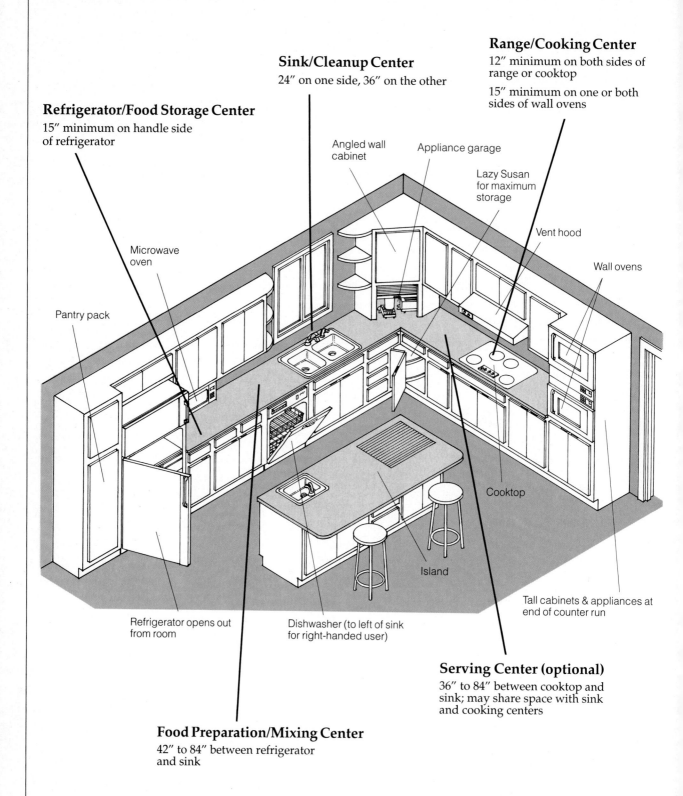

Refrigerator/Food Storage Center
15″ minimum on handle side
of refrigerator

Sink/Cleanup Center
24″ on one side, 36″ on the other

Range/Cooking Center
12″ minimum on both sides of
range or cooktop

15″ minimum on one or both
sides of wall ovens

Angled wall
cabinet

Appliance garage

Lazy Susan
for maximum
storage

Vent hood

Wall ovens

Microwave
oven

Pantry pack

Cooktop

Refrigerator opens out
from room

Dishwasher (to left of sink
for right-handed user)

Island

Tall cabinets & appliances at
end of counter run

Serving Center (optional)
36″ to 84″ between cooktop and
sink; may share space with sink
and cooking centers

Food Preparation/Mixing Center
42″ to 84″ between refrigerator
and sink

MAPPING THE FIVE WORK CENTERS

The real key to planning an efficient kitchen layout is to concentrate on the five work centers, allowing for both adequate countertop space and storage in each area.

Listed below (and shown on the facing page) are guidelines for planning each center. These rules are not absolute, and in very small or oddly shaped spaces you'll need to compromise. Adjacent centers may share space. Corners don't count—you can't stand in front of them.

As a rule, items should be stored in the *area of first use*. The one exception? Everyday dishes and flatware: store them near the *point of last use*—the dishwasher or sink.

Refrigerator/food storage center. Allow at least 15 inches of countertop space on the handle side of the refrigerator as a landing area for groceries. Ideally, the refrigerator is at the end of a cabinet run, near the access door, with the door rotating out. (Need to place the refrigerator inside a cabinet run? Think about a built-in, side-by-side model.)

Also consider an 18- or 21-inch drawer unit (see pages 62–69 for more on cabinets). A smaller unit is too narrow to be useful, and 24-inch or larger drawers will almost inevitably fill up with junk.

An over-the-refrigerator cabinet is a good bet for infrequently used items. Custom pullouts or a stock "pantry pack" are a hit for the tall, narrow spot flanking the refrigerator.

Sink/cleanup center. Figure a minimum of 24 inches of counter space on one side of the sink and 36 inches on the other. (If you're planning a second, smaller sink elsewhere, those clearances can be less.) It's best to locate the sink and cleanup center between the refrigerator and range or cooktop.

Traditionally, designers place the dishwasher for a right-hander to the left of the sink area and to the right for a lefty. But do whatever makes *you* comfortable. Consider the location in relation to your serving center (see at right).

Plan to store cleaning supplies in the sink area. A large variety of bins and pullouts—both built-ins and retrofits—are available for undersink storage. Tilt-down fronts for sponges and other supplies are available on many sink base cabinets.

Range/cooking center. You'll need at least 12 inches of countertop area on each side of the range or cooktop as a landing area for hot pots and casseroles, and to allow pot handles to be turned to the sides while pots are in use. If the cooktop is on an island or peninsula, the same rule applies.

You also should allow 15 inches of countertop on one or both sides of a wall oven. Typically, stacked wall ovens are at the end of a cabinet run; if they're in the middle, allow 15 inches on both sides.

Although we think of a microwave oven as part of the cooking center, many people prefer it near the refrigerator/freezer or in the serving center. Mount the microwave inside an oven cabinet, on the underside of a wall cabinet, or just below the countertop in a base run or an island.

Plan to store frequently used pots and pans in base pullout drawers mounted on heavy-duty, full-extension drawer guides.

Food preparation/mixing center. This auxiliary center is ideally located between the refrigerator and sink; plan a minimum of 42 inches of countertop, a maximum of 84 inches. Although it may not be a good idea to raise or lower countertop heights (if you have an eye toward resale, that is), the food preparation area is a good place to customize. A marble counter insert is a boon for the serious pastry chef.

Appliance garages with tambour or paneled doors are still popular in this area. (Be sure to add electrical outlets in the recess.) Need a place for spices or staples? An open shelf or backsplash rack provides a nice accent.

Serving center. If you have space, locate this optional work center between the range and sink if possible; size it between 36 and 84 inches (remember, you can share space here with both cleanup and cooking centers).

Everyday dishes, glassware, flatware, serving plates, and bowls, as well as napkins and placemats belong in this area. The dishwasher should be nearby; some models even have integral trays that can be placed right into the flatware drawer.

THREE AUXILIARY CENTERS

Three additional kitchen options have become so popular that they are quickly gaining unofficial work center status: the breakfast/dining area, the menu planning/office center, and the built-in pantry or wine cellar. Before solidifying your plans, think about whether or not you wish to include one or more of these areas.

Cabinet & Appliance Cutouts

To visualize possible layouts, first photocopy these scale outlines and cut them out. Move the cutouts around on a tracing of your floor plan (drawn to the same scale). Then draw the shapes onto the plan. It's easy to make your own cutouts for specialized appliances and other features.

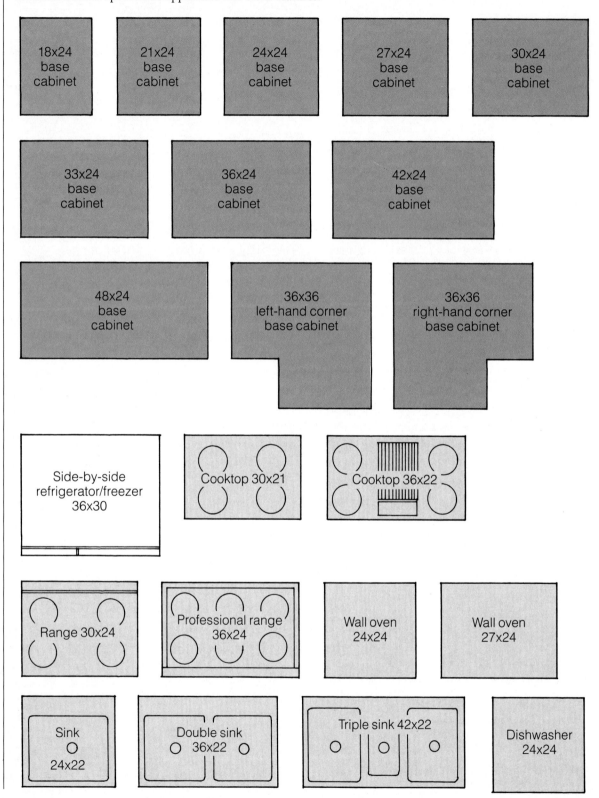

HEIGHTS & CLEARANCES

As shown at top right, there are standard minimum clearances in a well-planned kitchen. These dimensions ensure enough space for both busy cook and occasional cookie monsters; enough door clearance for free access to cabinets, dishwasher, and refrigerator; and enough traffic lanes for diners to comfortably enter and exit a breakfast nook.

Shown at bottom right are standard depths and heights for base and wall cabinets and shelves, plus recommended heights for stools, menu-planning desk, and eating counters.

TURNING CORNERS

Corners are the number one problem when planning cabinet runs. Two cabinets simply butted together waste storage space in the corner: on a base run, this adds up to a 24- by 24-inch waste; above, it's a 12-inch by 12-inch waste.

Angled cabinets, blind cabinets, corner sinks, and lazy Susans all offer corner solutions. For details on these units, see pages 66–67.

WINDOW OVER THE SINK?

The classic kitchen configuration nearly always centered the sink below a window. But how many hours do busy pot scrubbers spend looking out the window? How often is it light when you're working at the sink? Many of today's kitchen designers feel there's no real reason to place the sink below an existing window; on the other hand, consider it. It does bother most people to have the sink near a window but not quite under it.

SOFFITS: OPEN OR CLOSED?

Another decision you or your designer will have to make is what to do with the *soffit* area—the space between a typical wall cabinet (84 inches top line) and the ceiling (96 inches or higher). Should you leave it open? Add open shelves or rails for china and other collectibles? Close it in with framing and wallboard? Extend wall cabinets to the ceiling? Or build a box soffit out over the wall cabinets and add downlights for task lighting? Your soffit choice will help determine the overall look and feel of your kitchen.

Need a crash course on style and design? Simply turn the page.

Standard Kitchen Dimensions

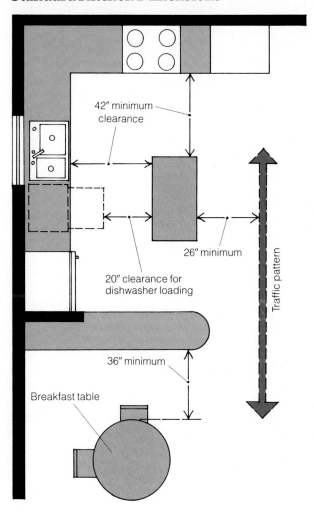

42" minimum clearance

26" minimum

20" clearance for dishwasher loading

36" minimum

Breakfast table

Traffic pattern

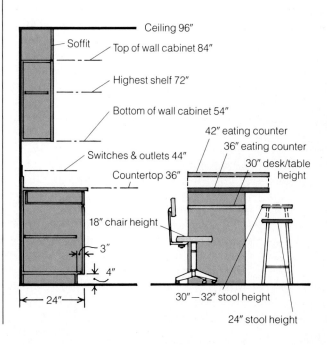

Ceiling 96"
Soffit
Top of wall cabinet 84"
Highest shelf 72"
Bottom of wall cabinet 54"
42" eating counter
36" eating counter
30" desk/table height
Switches & outlets 44"
Countertop 36"
18" chair height
3"
4"
24"
30"–32" stool height
24" stool height

LINE, SHAPE & SCALE

Three visual keys to planning a balanced, pleasing kitchen design are line, shape, and scale. You'll need to consider each of these elements—plus color, texture, and pattern—to achieve the overall look you want.

Looking at lines. Most kitchens incorporate many different types of lines—vertical, horizontal, diagonal, curved, and angular—but often one predominates and characterizes the design. Vertical lines give a sense of height, horizontal lines add width, diagonals suggest movement, and curved and angular lines impart a feeling of grace and dynamism.

Continuity of lines gives a sense of unity to a design. Try an elevation sketch of your proposed kitchen. How do the vertical lines created by the base cabinets, windows, doors, wall cabinets, and appliances fit together? It's not necessary for them to align perfectly, but you should consider such changes as varying the width of a wall cabinet (without sacrificing storage) to line it up with the range, sink, or corresponding base cabinet.

You can follow a similar process to smooth out horizontal lines. Does the top of the window match the top of the wall cabinets? If the window is just a few inches higher, you can either raise the cabinets or add trim and a soffit. If you're including a wall oven, align its bottom with the counter or its top with the bottom of the adjacent wall cabinet.

Studying shapes. Take a look at the shapes created by doorways, windows, cabinets, appliances, peninsulas, islands, and other elements in your kitchen. If these shapes are different, is there a basic sense of harmony? If you have an arch over a cooking niche, for example, you may want to repeat that shape in a doorway, on raised-panel cabinet doors, or in the trim of an open shelf. Or you can complement an angled peninsula by adding an angled corner cabinet or cooktop unit on the diagonally opposite wall.

Weighing the scale. When the scale of kitchen elements is proportionate to the overall scale of the kitchen, the design appears harmonious. A small kitchen seems even smaller if fitted with large appliances and expanses of closed cabinets. Open shelves, large windows, and a simple overall design visually enlarge such a room.

Consider the proportions of adjacent elements as well. Smaller objects arranged in a group help balance a larger item, making it less obtrusive.

RIDING THE COLOR WHEEL

The size and orientation of your kitchen, your personal preferences, and the mood you want to create all affect the selection of your color scheme. Light colors reflect light, making walls recede; thus a small kitchen appears more spacious.

A Sample Elevation

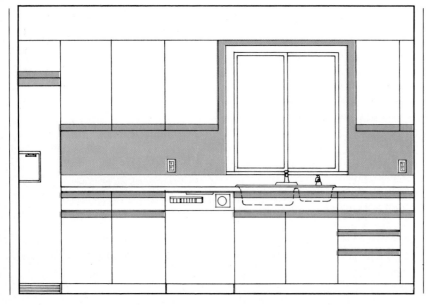

Alignment of vertical and horizontal lines creates a harmonious design. In the sample drawing at left, verticals match up between base and wall cabinets; refrigerator and surrounding storage are incorporated into the flow. A built-in soffit fills the area above wall cabinets and, along with sleek pull bars on cabinets, promotes a smooth horizontal look.

Dark colors absorb light and can visually lower a ceiling or shorten a narrow room.

When considering colors for a small kitchen, remember that too much contrast has the same effect as a dark color: it reduces the sense of space. Contrasting colors work well for adding accents or drawing attention to interesting structural elements, but if you want to conceal a problem feature, it's best to use one color throughout the area.

Depending on the orientation of your kitchen, you may want to use warm or cool colors to balance the quality of light. While oranges, yellows, or colors with a red tone impart a feeling of warmth, they also contract space. Blues, greens, or colors with a blue tone make an area seem cool—and larger.

A light, monochromatic color scheme (using different shades of one color) is restful and serene. Contrasting colors, on the other hand, add vibrancy and excitement to a design; however, a color scheme with contrasting colors may be overpowering unless the tones of the colors are varied. Another possibility is to include bright, intense accent colors in furnishings and accessories that can be changed without too much trouble or cost.

Remember that the color temperature and intensity, as well as placement of any light fixtures, will have an effect on overall color rendition; for details, see pages 91–93.

TEXTURE & PATTERN

Textures and patterns work like color in defining a room's space and style. The kitchen's surface materials may include many different textures—from a shiny tile backsplash to rough oak cabinets or a quarry tile floor.

Rough textures absorb light, make colors dull, and lend a feeling of informality. Smooth textures reflect light and suggest elegance or modernity. Using similar textures helps unify a design and create a mood.

Pattern choices must harmonize with the predominant style of the room. Although we usually associate pattern with wall coverings or a cabinet finish, even natural substances such as wood, brick, or stone create patterns.

While variety in texture and pattern adds interest, too much variety can be overwhelming. It's best to let a strong feature or dominating pattern be the focus of your design and choose other surfaces to complement rather than compete with it.

Designing with Color

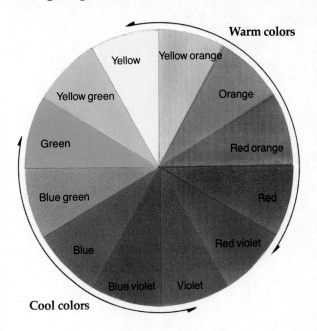

As a rule, work with adjacent colors on the color wheel; save complementary colors—those opposite one another—for accents.

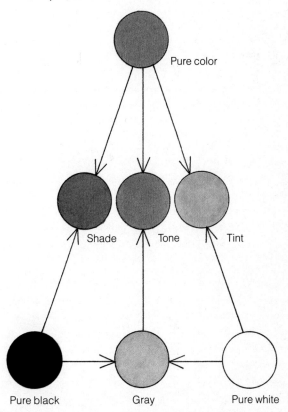

The pyramid illustrates the variation of hues: shades are made by adding black to pure color, tones by adding gray, and tints by adding white. Gray combines pure black and pure white.

Structural Framing

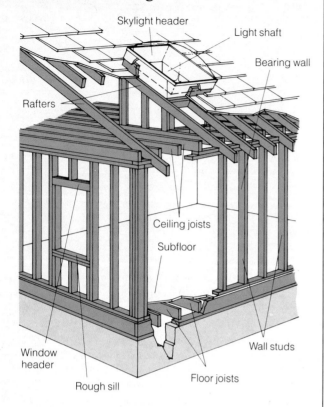

Skylight header

Light shaft

Bearing wall

Rafters

Ceiling joists

Subfloor

Window header

Wall studs

Rough sill

Floor joists

Plumbing

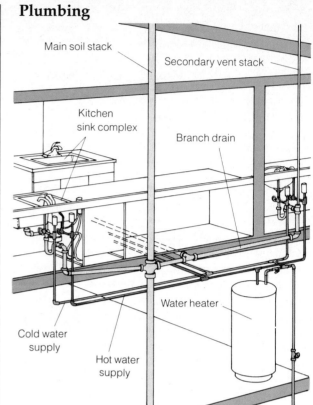

Main soil stack

Secondary vent stack

Kitchen sink complex

Branch drain

Cold water supply

Hot water supply

Water heater

STRUCTURAL CHANGES

Are you planning to open up space, add a skylight, or lay a heavy stone floor? If so, your kitchen remodel may require some structural alterations.

As shown above, walls may be either *bearing* (supporting the weight of ceiling joists and/or second-story walls) or *nonbearing*. If you're removing all or part of a bearing wall, you must "bridge" the spot with a sturdy beam and posts. Nonbearing (also called *partition*) walls can usually be removed without too much trouble—unless there are pipes or wires routed through the area.

Doors and windows require special framing as shown—the size of the header depends on the width of the opening and your local building codes. Skylights require similar cuts through ceiling joists and/or rafters.

Planning a vaulted or cathedral ceiling instead of ceiling covering and joists? You'll probably need a few beams to maintain the structural integrity.

Hardwood, ceramic tile, or stone floors require a very stiff underlayment. Solution? Beef up the floor joists and/or add additional plywood or particleboard subflooring on top.

PLUMBING RESTRICTIONS

Suppose you wish to move the sink to the other side of the room or add a kitchen island with a vegetable sink or wet bar?

Generally, it's an easy job—at least conceptually—to extend existing hot and cold water supply pipes to a new sink or appliance. The exception? When you're working on a concrete slab foundation. In this case, you'll need to drill through the slab or bring the pipes through the wall from another point above floor level.

Every house has a main soil stack. Below the level of the fixtures, it's your home's primary drainpipe; at its upper end, which protrudes through the roof, the stack becomes a vent. A proposed fixture located within a few feet of the main stack usually can be drained and vented directly by the stack. In some areas a new island sink can be wet-vented (using an oversize branch drain as both drain and vent), but this is illegal in other areas. Sometimes a fixture located far from the main stack will require its own branch drain and a secondary vent stack of its own rising to the roof. The moral? Be sure to check your local plumbing codes for exact requirements.

Electrical Wiring

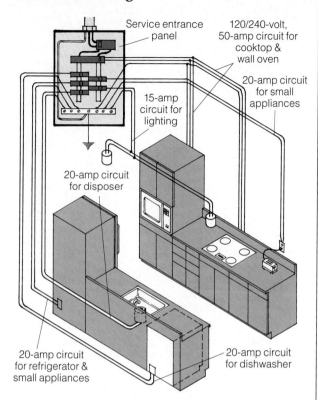

Service entrance panel

120/240-volt, 50-amp circuit for cooktop & wall oven

20-amp circuit for small appliances

15-amp circuit for lighting

20-amp circuit for disposer

20-amp circuit for refrigerator & small appliances

20-amp circuit for dishwasher

Mechanical Systems

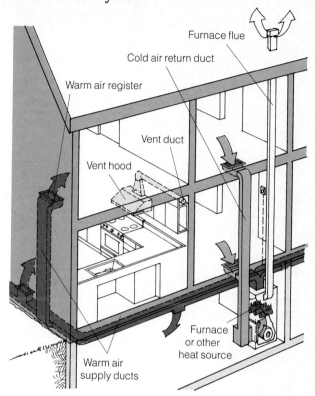

Furnace flue

Cold air return duct

Warm air register

Vent duct

Vent hood

Furnace or other heat source

Warm air supply ducts

ELECTRICAL REQUIREMENTS

Electrical capacity is probably the number one oversight of most homeowners aiming to remodel. All those shiny new appliances take a lot of power to operate! In fact, the typical kitchen makeover requires three to five new circuits.

Requirements for electrical circuits serving a modern kitchen and dining area are clearly prescribed by the National Electrical Code (NEC). Plug-in outlets and switches for small appliances and the refrigerator must be served by a minimum of two 20-amp circuits. Light fixtures share one or more 15-amp circuits, which also run, as a rule, to the dining room, living room, or other adjacent space.

If you're installing a dishwasher and/or disposer, you'll need a separate 20-amp circuit for each. Most electric ranges use an individual 50-amp, 120/240-volt major appliance circuit. Wall ovens and a separate cooktop may share a 50-amp circuit.

Older homes with two-wire (120 volts only) service of less than 100 amps simply can't support many major improvements. To add a new oven or dishwasher you may need to increase your service type and rating, which means updating the service entrance equipment.

MECHANICAL SYSTEMS

Air-conditioning, heating, and ventilation systems may all be affected by your proposed kitchen remodel. Changes will be governed either by your local plumbing regulations or a separate mechanical code.

Both air-conditioning and heating ducts are relatively easy to reroute, as long as you can gain access from a basement, crawl space, garage wall, or unfinished attic. Radiant-heat pipes or other slab-embedded systems may pose problems; check them out. Registers are usually easy to reposition; the toespace area of base cabinets is a favorite spot these days for retrofits. (You can also buy hydronic or electric space heaters designed for these areas.) Don't place any cold air returns in the new kitchen.

Are you planning a new freestanding range, a cooktop, wall ovens, or a built-in barbecue? You'll need to "think ventilation"—either a hood above or a downdraft system exiting through the floor or an exterior wall. The more discreet downdraft system is especially apt for a new kitchen island or peninsula, but vent hoods can add an attractive focal point to some design schemes. See pages 82–83 for more details on ventilation principles and options.

DOLLARS & CENTS

How much will your new kitchen cost? According to the National Kitchen & Bath Association, the average figure is $17,803; in the West it climbs to $22,986. These are, of course, only the sketchiest of estimates. You may simply need to replace countertops, add recessed downlights, reface your cabinets, or exchange a worn-out range to achieve the results you're after. On the other hand, the sky is the limit: extensive structural changes coupled with ultra-high-end materials and appliances can easily add up to $100,000.

As shown below, kitchen cabinets typically eat up 37 percent of the pie; labor comes in at around 20 percent; and, on the average, appliances add another 19 percent. Structural, plumbing, and electrical changes all affect the bottom line significantly.

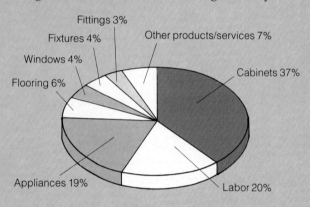

Fittings 3%
Fixtures 4%
Windows 4%
Flooring 6%
Other products/services 7%
Cabinets 37%
Appliances 19%
Labor 20%

How do you keep the budget under control? For starters, know if you're looking at a simple face-lift, a more extensive replacement, or a major structural remodel. Both cabinet and appliance prices vary drastically, depending on whether they're low-, middle-, high-, or ultra-high-end. Shop for ballpark figures in different categories, mull them over, then present your architect or designer with a range of options and a bottom line you're comfortable with.

And what about the cost and criteria for selection of architects and designers you'll work with? Expect to be charged either a flat fee or a percentage of the total cost of the goods purchased (usually 8 to 10 percent). General contractors will work their fee into a final bid. Don't make price your only criterion for selection, however; quality of work, reliability, rapport, and on-time performance are also important. Ask professionals for the names and phone numbers of recent clients. Call several and ask them how happy they were with the process and the results. You may want to ask if you can inspect the work.

WORKING WITH PROFESSIONALS

The listing below covers professionals in kitchen design and construction and delineates the fine points (although there's overlap) between architects, designers, contractors, and other design and construction professionals.

Architects. Architects are state-licensed professionals with degrees in architecture. They're trained to create designs that are structurally sound, functional, and aesthetically pleasing. They also know construction materials, can negotiate bids from contractors, and can supervise the actual work. Many architects are members of the American Institute of Architects (AIA). If stress calculations must be made, architects can make them; other professionals need state-licensed engineers to design the structure and sign the working drawings.

So is an architect the number one choice for designing your kitchen? Maybe yes, maybe no. If your new remodel involves major structural changes, an architect should be consulted. But some architects may not be as familiar with the latest in kitchen design and materials as other specialists may be.

Kitchen designers. A kitchen designer is a specialist in kitchens. These individuals are often well-informed about the latest trends in furnishings and appliances, but they may have neither the structural knowledge of the architect nor the aesthetic skill of a good interior designer (see facing page).

If you're working with a kitchen designer, look for a member of the National Kitchen & Bath Association (NKBA) or a Certified Kitchen Designer (CKD). Each association has a code of ethics and a continuing program to inform members about the latest building materials and techniques.

What about other so-called "kitchen specialists"? (These may include showroom personnel, building center staff, or other retailers.) Some are quite qualified, but some may simply be there to sell you more goods. The decision depends on your scope: if your kitchen needs only a minor facelift, this help may be just what you need; if the job is major, check the specialist's qualifications carefully.

Typically, you provide a rough floor plan and fill out a questionnaire; the retailer provides a finished plan and/or materials list—if you buy the cabinets or other goods. Some firms do the work via computer simulation; others the traditional way.

Interior designers. Even if you're working with an architect or kitchen designer, you may wish to call on the services of an interior designer for finishing touches. These experts specialize in the decorating and furnishing of rooms and can offer fresh, innovative ideas and advice. Through their contacts, a homeowner has access to materials and products not available at the retail level. Many designers belong to the American Society of Interior Designers (ASID), a professional organization.

As kitchen design becomes more sophisticated, professionals become more specialized. A prime example is the lighting design field, which has come into its own in recent years. Lighting designers specify fixtures and placement of the lighting for your new kitchen and work with the contractor or an installer to make the new lighting scheme a reality.

General contractors. Contractors specialize in construction, although some also have design skills and experience as well. General contractors may do all the work themselves, or they may assume responsibility for hiring qualified subcontractors, ordering construction materials, and seeing that the job is completed according to contract. Contractors can also secure building permits and arrange for inspections as work progresses.

When choosing a contractor, ask architects, designers, and friends for recommendations. To compare bids, contact at least three state-licensed contractors; give each one either an exact description and your own sketches of the desired remodeling or plans and specifications prepared by an architect or designer. Include a detailed account of who will be responsible for what work.

Subcontractors. If you act as your own contractor, you will have to hire and supervise subcontractors for specialized jobs such as wiring, plumbing, or tiling. You'll be responsible for permits, insurance, and payroll taxes, as well as direct supervision of all the aspects of construction. Do you have the time or the knowledge required for the job? Be sure to assess your energy level carefully!

Warm and woody, or sleek and stark: the choice is yours. At top right, butcher-block tops and copper pots blend with clean white cabinets and classic gas range. Below, unexpected angles, gleaming granite, and slate floor set off ultramodern cabinets and appliances.

A PLANNING PRIMER **21**

CASE STUDIES

I n the old days, a picture was worth a thousand words. And regardless of the current exchange rate, photos are still the best way to show what's new in kitchen design.

Stylewise, these eighteen studies present as broad a palette as possible. You'll find European cabinets and components, French country motifs, polished colonial brass, high-tech concrete, and stainless steel. But don't worry too much about sticking to one theme: creative kitchens often combine elements of several standard styles.

Each real-life situation is a little different, too. Some of these kitchens are large; others are small. Most of the designs address special problems or requests—hopefully, one of these solutions will work for you. If it's individual pieces that catch your fancy, you'll find more details in Chapter 3, "A Shopper's Guide."

In vivid contrast to ultramodern cabinet layouts, this conservatory kitchen sports the "unfitted" look, based on finely crafted freestanding pieces. An ash-and-maple work table wraps around the central column; pot rack and dish rack show off their wares; a freestanding cupboard at the far end of the room handles pantry chores.

VIEW THROUGH THE ARCH

How can you expand a tiny galley kitchen? To obtain space, this architect first eliminated a small bathroom in back, then added an arch at the entry to the adjacent dining room, and finally opened up the view into the adjoining family room via an angled peninsula.

European-style white cabinets set the tone; curved end cabinets imitate the fluid shapes of the peninsula, soffits, vent hood, and Italian light fixtures. The custom vent hood gleams with polished brass and mirrored steel. Plenty of pullouts, appliance garages, and lazy Susans make storage a breeze—there's even a sealed pullout bin for dog food!

Architect: J. Allen Sayles/Architectural Kitchens & Baths.

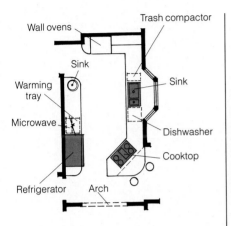

The view from the dining room arch (left) includes high-gloss cabinets, blue Brazilian granite countertops, an imposing brass and stainless steel vent hood, and Italian light fixtures that repeat the granite's color. The sink area (shown above) looks out on a soothing garden view; the angled peninsula (right) houses modular gas and barbecue cooktop components and provides a casual eating counter.

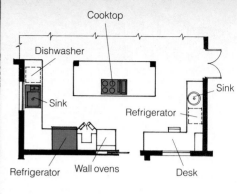

Cooktop

Dishwasher

Sink

Sink

Refrigerator

Refrigerator

Wall ovens

Desk

COZY, COMFORTABLE GREAT ROOM

The big, high-ceilinged living room was too cold and formal for the homeowners who wanted a comfortable, cozy space for everyday relaxing. To solve the problem, they pushed out the wall next to the original kitchen and created a great room to house many of their various activities. Beams, cabinetry, and decor link the areas visually.

The basic kitchen L includes stacked wall ovens, a built-in refrigerator, and a stainless steel sink; a large central island houses a modular cooktop ensemble and plenty of storage compartments. Downdraft ventilation preserves the open feel. A built-in desk holds down one corner; a wine bar area completes the picture.

Architect: William B. Remick.

Views from the large central island include a sitting and entertainment area (left) and a window seat and dining nook (above). Custom-crafted, stained-birch cabinets (facing page, top left) harmonize with mahogany floor; solid-surface countertops accent both basic kitchen L and island. Wine bar's hand-painted backsplash tiles (facing page, top center) are a modern match for originals discovered when the old kitchen was torn out.

COUNTRY COOKING

Out went the old walls and in came a new kitchen that meets the needs of a serious cook. The new maple butcher-block island is the center for food preparation; pots on the striking pot rack provide a focal point. A residential/commercial range (insulated for home use) puts out plenty of BTUs; the mirrored wall oven with a pizza insert and the warming tray below complete the cooking center.

The style is clean country contemporary: black granite countertops accent the white, glossy, raised-panel cabinets; the silver and black of appliances add punch. Backsplashes are white field tiles with black diamond accents. Lighting is from PAR downlights with strip undercabinet lighting for close tasks. A new bay window and built-in window seat area complete the far end of the new space.

Architect: Willliam E. Cullen.

The shiny range, wall oven, and warming tray (top) form the heart of the cooking center. Pullout shelves (bottom) make optimum use of "beside-the-refrigerator" space. The tile backsplash (right) matches the enameled cabinets and granite countertops; the glow comes from strip lights behind the wall cabinet valance.

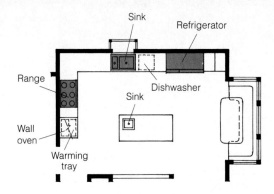

Sink

Refrigerator

Range

Dishwasher

Sink

Wall oven

Warming tray

The kitchen island (below) is the heart of this study in black and white: the butcher-block top provides plenty of surface for food preparation, and shelves hold racks of bulk ingredients and spices. A work triangle wraps around the island; pots are close at hand and provide a striking accent. The rack was constructed from two commercial units.

LIFE IN THE CLOUDS

The arched ceiling and beautiful faux-finished surfaces give an irresistible floating feeling to this kitchen. Glass pendant fixtures lead the eye downward and illuminate the central island.

Cabinets are bleached ash, lacquered here and there for accent. The residential-commercial range is backed with light-filtering glass block and limestone tiles, repeating the limestone of the floor.

Faux-finished cabinets for flatware and glasses line the attached butler's pantry; an additional sink and dishwasher handle major entertaining.

Designer: Agnes Bourne.

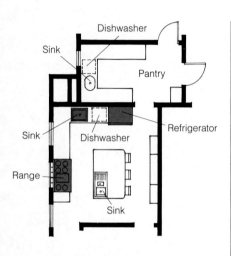

The compact kitchen (facing page) blends bleached ash cabinets with sky-blue and green faux painting and soft limestone. The dark green range (above) has limestone and glass-block backsplash; the original vent hood was repainted to match the ceiling. A butler's pantry (left) has storage aplenty and room to handle serious cleanup tasks.

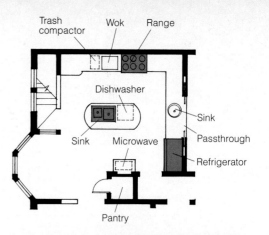

Diamond shapes are everywhere:
in the drawer and door pulls; in the
range backsplash and vent hood; in
the etched-glass wall cabinets and
passthrough doors; in the granite-tile
counter backsplash; even in the custom
glass-and-copper light fixtures.

A STUDY IN DIAMONDS

The homeowners wanted a new, larger kitchen that also had to say *avant-garde*. The kitchen style evolved as both clients and designers started with a diamond motif, liked it in copper, then chose mahogany to complement the copper.

Indeed, copper and mahogany abound. To complete the look, the range area has a shiny quilted-steel backsplash; oak floors have mahogany strip inserts following the island and room outline; walls and ceiling bays are finished with a pale faux-finish paint. A skylight is concealed in one ceiling bay.

But this kitchen works hard, too. At the heart of the cooking area is a professional, six-burner gas range; an electric wok is located just to the left. The large, granite-covered island with its double stainless steel sink is accessible from both cooktop and microwave; the pass-through area has a second sink.

Designer: Osburn Design.

Across the island from the range area, a handsome custom cabinet (right) houses both microwave and plenty of related storables. Etched-glass pocket doors open to create a passthrough to the dining room. Quilted steel and copper set off range area (above top). Granite-tile backsplash (above bottom) has small black tile accents; under-cabinet warm fluorescent lights provide task lighting.

PINING FOR THE COUNTRY

The massive stone chimney was all that remained from a devastating fire; after sandblasting, it became the center around which the new kitchen and living space revolved.

In the kitchen, knotty pine cabinets, strip oak flooring, and bright cobalt blue tiles evoke the country theme. The cooktop area is the center of attention; sink and dining areas occupy opposite ends; and a breakfast peninsula adjoins the sink area.

Pine roof decking towers over all, supported by sturdy beams and iron framing ties. Bay windows at both ends, plus a skylight high in the ceiling, bring in daylight; when night falls, downlights, tracks, and Italian halogen pendants take over.

Designer: Wally Brueske/Design Cabinet Showrooms.

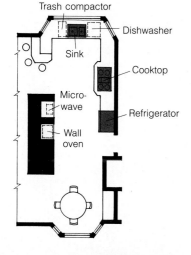

Looking left from the front door, the tiled cooktop area and vent hood (facing page) are the first things to grab your eye. The wall oven and microwave (upper left) are new additions to the massive stone wall; the breakfast nook (lower left) has a cozy, built-in feel and displays a striking pendant fixture. Track fixtures (above) shine down on pine, oak, and an iron pot rack.

LOOKING FOR LIGHT

The owners of this small windowless kitchen had two priorities: first, they wanted European styling and efficiency; second, they wanted to create a feeling of light.

The solution was to combine pale gray laminate cabinets and sleek white appliances, hard-working pullouts and lazy Susans for storables, black countertops, and diamond-accented vinyl flooring. Custom tile work was added for contrast.

As a final touch, these components were mixed with effective lighting: low-voltage mono-tracks and 120-volt downlights for general light, undercabinet fluorescents for countertop tasks, and halogen downlights for punch.

General contractor: Iris Harrell.

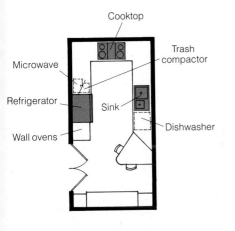

The view over the breakfast peninsula (above) shows the main kitchen, the diamond motif on the vinyl floor, and the cooktop backsplash. The cooktop area (facing page) has a custom stainless hood and modular cooktop; a mirrored storage wall (top left) and etched glass doors (bottom left) lend a light, open look to this small space.

HOME ON THE RANGE

Cows amble amiably through the wide-open spaces of this Southwestern kitchen. Subdued floor and countertop tiles, plus whitewashed pine cabinets, set the background; the oxydized copper vent hood, island lights, and green cabinet pulls provide gentle accents; handpainted backsplash murals add a dab of primary color.

The custom skylight and a large hanging fixture form the central point around which the kitchen revolves. To one side of the U-shaped layout is the main sink with a window; in the center are the cooking and refrigerator areas; the third side houses wall ovens, an undercounter wine cooler, and plenty of storage space. The island bridges each work center and serves as a breakfast counter; the formal dining table lies beyond.

Designer: Geoffrey Frost/Kitchen Studio Los Angeles.

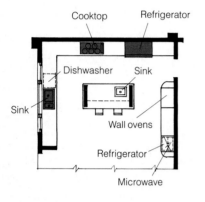

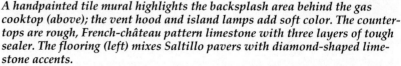

A handpainted tile mural highlights the backsplash area behind the gas cooktop (above); the vent hood and island lamps add soft color. The countertops are rough, French-château pattern limestone with three layers of tough sealer. The flooring (left) mixes Saltillo pavers with diamond-shaped limestone accents.

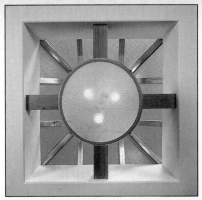

The U-shaped kitchen (below) is augmented by an island with a breakfast counter; the dining table is in the foreground. Day or night, a custom skylight and pendant fixture (right) provide touches of ambient light.

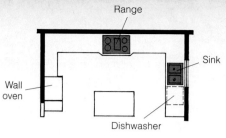

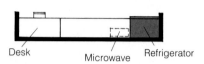

Range

Sink

Wall oven

Dishwasher

Desk

Microwave

Refrigerator

A handy wine rack (left) nestles into the end of the base cabinet run, showing the same attention to detail as the rest of the kitchen. The dishwasher's carved front panel harmonizes with the surrounding cabinets.

VERY FRENCH, VERY MODERN

Curved lines, ceiling beams, and a recurring fleur-de-lis motif are all indicators of the French country look. Here, handcarved distressed cabinets strike the theme; boxed beams, carved valances, and wood wainscoting repeat the motif. Handpainted tiles add color to countertops and backsplash areas; floor tiles are French limestone.

Attention to fine points is also a part of this style, and these cabinets provide great storage and display potential along with their furniture-like detailing. A freestanding island table adds counter space while emphasizing the overall country feel.

The gas range, wall oven, double sink, and dishwasher are all white, the perfect modern backdrop for old-world accents.

Designer: Garry Bishop/Showcase Kitchens.

Handcarved distressed cabinetry invokes the French country style; the main U-shaped area (shown at left) has contrasting handpainted tile on the countertops and range backsplash, plus French limestone flooring. Modern white appliances maintain the clean color palette. The wall cabinet detail (above) reveals several furniture-like touches: curved-panel door frames, a wine glass rack, and slatted dish dividers.

The central island (below) dominates the kitchen; it not only serves as a breakfast bar but integrates smoothly with each work center around the room. Side-by-side 30-inch ovens (left) are located opposite the cooktop; their size determined the width of the island.

TRADITIONAL CHERRY

Frame-and-panel is the style, cherry is the substance, in this well-appointed formal kitchen. Beautiful detailed cabinets provide plenty of specialized storage and house a cornucopia of conveniences: a six-burner gas cooktop with built-in vent hood; an integral-bowl main sink and brass bar sink; matching microwaves; and a built-in, side-by-side refrigerator. White solid-surface countertops add a light-colored accent.

In the center, a massive granite-topped island houses an extra refrigerator, undercounter freezer, and matching side-by-side wall ovens opposite the cooktop. Saltillo tile flooring softens the space and matches the paving on the adjacent veranda.

Designer: Bob Seger/Kitchens & Baths of Carmel.

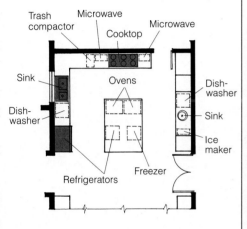

The wet bar area (left) features a shiny brass sink, its own dishwasher, a built-in icemaker, and lots of pullout storage. The main sink area (shown above) features an integral solid-surface bowl, an arched window, and dual appliance garages.

REFLECTIONS IN BLACK

European detailing shines throughout this bold, black kitchen. Floor-to-ceiling cabinets are aspen with semiopaque stain; many coats of clear polyester create the sparkle. Black appliance panels and mirrored backsplash continue the theme—even the existing refrigerator was painted black.

Bullnosed butcher-block countertops, sealed with polyurethane, cut through the black. The peninsula overhang doubles as an eating counter and divides the kitchen from an adjacent dining area. What appears to be strip flooring is really an oak-veneered "floating" system; it's laid over a foam base.

One word of warning: reflective surfaces can require a lot of care to keep spotless!

Designer: Plus Kitchens.

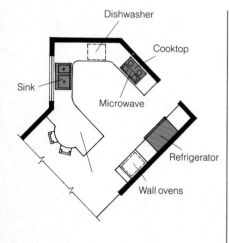

Black aspen cabinets with polyester coating provide the shine; butcher-block countertops and oak flooring add contrast. Kitchen angles provide interest; the lowered ceiling soffits and angled peninsula (right) accentuate the curves. A storage wall (above) wraps around the refrigerator and wall ovens, houses handy pullouts and bins. A low-voltage downlight shows off Italian collectibles inside the glass wall cabinet (left).

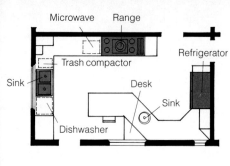

Microwave   Range

Trash compactor

Refrigerator

Sink

Desk

Sink

Dishwasher

OLD & NEW, WHITE & BLUE

This kitchen's design centered on two basic goals: to skillfully blend the remodel with the existing house style, and to showcase the brand new (but classic-looking) French range. White cabinets have fluting that mirrors the original dining room wainscoting. The blue and gold range and matching hood provide a burst of color; the original leaded glass windows have blue accents as well.

The kitchen's angled peninsula allows for a preparation area at one end and a well-appointed planning desk at the other. The random-plank flooring was stained, then sealed to match the dining room. Discreet downlights provide general illumination; strip lights below wall cabinets add task lighting

Architect: William B. Remick.

New cabinets, peninsula, and appliances blend with existing windows and styling (left). Base cabinets feature custom-crafted fluting, shaped from 1⅝-inch poplar; they support Spanish marble countertops. The kitchen's blue enamel and brass French range (above) has both high-powered gas and electric burners, as well as matching convection ovens. The planning center (facing page, top left) is nestled behind the angled peninsula. An original carved cabinet (facing page, top right) was built into an efficient wall unit.

TIGHT SPACE, EXPANSIVE STYLE

It took some fancy design work to turn this 6- by 13-foot city kitchen into something both visually exciting and highly functional. Bird's-eye maple cabinets, a faux finish, and granite tiles on the floor, countertop, and backsplash provide the punch. A double stainless steel sink and a window fill the short side; the refrigerator, dishwasher, and compact but efficient cooking center—including cooktop, microwave, and undercounter oven—complete the work triangle.

The existing door to the dining room was converted to a passthrough and the arch was added. Miniature track lights provide general illumination; strip lights above and below wall cabinets add both task and accent lighting.

Designer: Fontenot Designs.

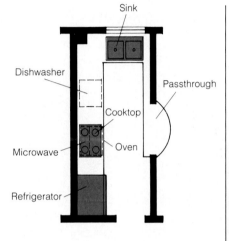

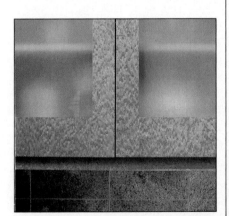

The view through the arch (facing page) highlights the new kitchen. Bird's-eye maple and frosted glass (top left) plus granite tiles provide new life for the narrow corridor (bottom left). The dining room (above) is an ideal spot to view the kitchen; faux finish ties the two rooms together.

A GATHERING PLACE

The family wanted a spot where they could be together—a place in keeping with the turn-of-the-century, formal style of the house. The designer transformed three original rooms into a kitchen, breakfast room, fireplace area, and office—all in one.

The large island defines the kitchen proper and provides plenty of food preparation space; a custom beveled skylight adds interest and brings in natural light. The sunny breakfast area has room for ten diners when the table is extended. Faux-finished walls echo green marble countertops and backsplashes; clean, cheery white highlights the ceiling, appliances, and cabinets. The floors are bleached oak.

Designer: Nan Rosenblatt.

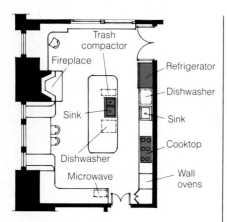

Visible from the island counter, the breakfast nook, or the office, this tile-clad fireplace unifies the kitchen area and offers plenty of room for wood storage. Angles match those throughout the room.

A study in white and green: plentiful natural light beams in on the kitchen area (below) and breakfast alcove (at right); faux finish on open walls and in soffit areas echoes the soft green marble countertops and back-splashes. White cabinets, ceiling, and appliances provide accent and maximize light.

Renovation of existing kitchen cabinets included restoring original brass pulls, clasps, and hinges (left).

Dishwasher Trash compactor

Sink Cooktop Sink

Ovens

Refrigerator Microwave Pantry

NEW LIFE FOR A COLONIAL KITCHEN

White paint, brass accents, and oak floors and trim add up to a classic revival for this colonial kitchen. The designers accepted the double challenge of preserving the integrity of the original design while adding the convenience of modern appliances and fixtures.

Most cabinets are original; others are faithful reproductions. Crown moldings, oak floors and countertop trim, white tile countertops, and lots of white paint complete the room. Modern lighting includes both downlights and undercabinet halogen strips.

The adjoining butler's pantry was a frequent inclusion in colonial houses. Here, the original cabinets have been refurbished; the brass sink and miniature track lights are new additions.

Designer: Bernadine Leach/Kitchens by Design.

New and old materials combine to refurbish a classic colonial beauty (left). The cabinets are original; the 30-inch ovens, sink, and faucet are up-to-the-minute new. White paint, oak, and additional brass on the vent hood and towel bars round out the picture. The butler's pantry (above) received the same loving care.

COUNTRY ELEGANCE

Although this kitchen means serious business, it's also a visual feast of colors and textures. Everywhere you look there's an elegant touch—a wash of blue, a plastered niche for cookware, a trompe l'oeil cabinet front, the gleam of neatly aligned stainless steel and copper pots. How might you categorize the look? The designers, brought in to help the owners pull things together, call it "French Shaker."

The kitchen has two long, narrow corridors defined by the lines of the sink and preparation table. Nearby is the main cooking alcove, equipped with a professional range, a gas barbecue, and a microwave. The granite-topped island—complete with a second sink and an overhanging buffet counter—continues the center line until the room steps down to a sunny "cafe" area.

Designer: Osburn Design.

Refrigerator
Sink
Warming tray
Dishwasher
Microwave
Warming alcove
Range
Barbecue
Sink

A skylight spills light onto the food preparation area (opposite page, top) and cooking alcove; dark woods blend with light faux-finished walls, stainless and copper pots, and a granite island countertop. The view past the blue-painted, concrete-basin sink area (opposite page, bottom) includes a beautiful clear-finished cabinet.

The wall niche (above) opposite the range and sink is partly decorative, partly for function: a radiant slab warms dishes ready to be served. The dining area (left) has plenty of sunshine, thanks to abundant windows and matching French doors.

NEW ORLEANS STYLE

Enchanted by the gracious ambience of New Orleans, owners of this home asked their architect to re-create it in their great room. A hammered tin ceiling, arched windows, twirling ceiling fans, and custom cherry units were used to evoke the warmth and spirit of the South.

In the kitchen, a large cherry-and-granite island with modular cooktop holds down center stage; a deep fryer provides firepower for beignets and other down-home dishes. Surrounding the island is a classic white kitchen, featuring raised-panel cabinets and laminate countertops.

Architect: J. Allen Sayles/Architectural Kitchens & Baths.

A solid cherry-and-granite island and towering vent hood (above) hold down the center of this white kitchen; the island style and finish match the living room and dining room pieces (left), emphasizing the great-room effect. The photo on the facing page, top left, offers a peek into the alcove between the wall oven and refrigerator. Between-studs storage space (facing page, top right) was re-created from the original kitchen.

A LOFTY SEASIDE PERCH

This home, which hovers above the rugged Pacific coast, mixes generous expanses of glass, wood, and concrete. The Japanese effect the owner wanted is evident in the natural fir poles, radiating beams, and cedar roof decking, as well as in the open plan of which the kitchen is a part.

In the kitchen area, charcoal-colored laminate cabinets and gray countertops blend with ceramic floor tiles and a massive concrete fireplace rising from the living room below; the island's wood edgings echo both window trim and roof decking. A granite-topped dining table commands the prime fireside location.

Architect: Mickey Muennig.

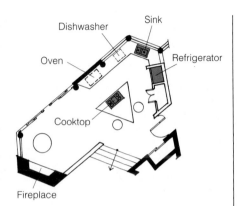

Hardwood stairs lead the eye from the living room up to the open kitchen (facing page), which revolves around a triangular central island and corresponding track fixture (above). The kitchen is bounded on one side by a freestanding refrigerator wall (top left), and on the dining side by a form-stamped concrete fireplace (bottom left).

A
SHOPPER'S
GUIDE

Frameless laminate cabinets, synthetic marble countertops, batch-feed garbage disposers, halogen cooktops, low-voltage wall washers—enough! The innocent kitchen shopper can be overwhelmed with the latest in gleaming stainless or blaring red components.

What are the current trends in kitchen design? That's where this chapter can help. To keep things simple, we've focused on one component at a time: cabinets, countertops, sinks, appliances, flooring, walls and ceilings, and light fixtures. Color photos show the latest styles; text and comparison charts will give you the working knowledge to brave the appliance center, to communicate with an architect or designer, or simply to replace that dingy old-fashioned countertop.

If you'd like manufacturers' names and addresses for many of the products we show, see the listings on pages 142–143.

The view past a detached coffee bar includes sleek black and stainless components, shiny granite countertops, and both natural and painted wood cabinets, walls, ceiling, and floor. Over the railing at right is the raised breakfast mezzanine. Architect: William B. Remick.

CABINETS

Cabinets are the key element in kitchen storage. They create the room's personality and provide the backbone for its organization. For this reason—and because they represent the largest single investment in a new kitchen—it is important to study the many options available before making the plunge.

What materials do you prefer? Your choices include warm hardwoods, sleek European-style laminates, and painted veneers. Will you buy stock cabinets at the local lumberyard, order custom modular units, or have cabinets handcrafted by a custom cabinetmaker?

On the following pages, we show you the two ways all cabinets are constructed and the three ways you can buy cabinets. We also describe the basic cabinet units and how they're modified and organized into a functional kitchen.

Traditional or European-style?

Traditional American cabinets mask the raw front edges of each box with a 1-by-2 "faceframe." Doors and drawers then fit in one of three ways: flush; partially offset, with a notch; or completely overlaying the frame.

Faceframe cabinets offer somewhat more flexibility in irregular spaces than modular ones do; the outer edges of the frame can be

The three cabinet styles on the facing page may look different, but they're all examples of European, or frameless, construction. "Traditional" pine cabinets at top left aren't really frame-and-panel—they have one-piece routed doors. The bright red, curved units (top right) are high-gloss laminate. The maple cabinets (bottom) are truly custom—ebony and mahogany inlays create an accordion effect.

planed and shaped (called "scribing") to conform to unique discrepancies. Since the frame covers it up, thinner or lower-quality wood can be used in the sides (thus reducing price). But the frame takes up space; it reduces the size of the door opening, so drawers or slide-out accessories must be significantly smaller than the width of the cabinet.

Europeans, whose kitchens are so tiny that all space counts, came up with "frameless" cabinets. A simple narrow trim strip covers raw edges, which butt directly against each other. Doors and drawers fit usually to within ¼ inch of each other, revealing a thin sliver of the trim. Interior components—such as drawers—can be sized larger, practically to the full dimension of the box.

Another big difference: Frameless cabinets typically have a separate toespace pedestal, or plinth. This allows you to set counter heights specifically to your liking, stack base units, or make use of space at floor level.

Thanks to absolute standardization of every component, frameless cabinets are unsurpassed in versatility. Precise columns of holes are drilled on the inside faces. These holes are generally in the same places, no matter what cabinets you buy, and components just plug right into them.

The terms "system 32" and "32-millimeter" refer to the basic matrix of all these cabinets: all the holes, hinge fittings, cabinet joints, and mounts are set 32 millimeters apart.

Cabinet Closeups

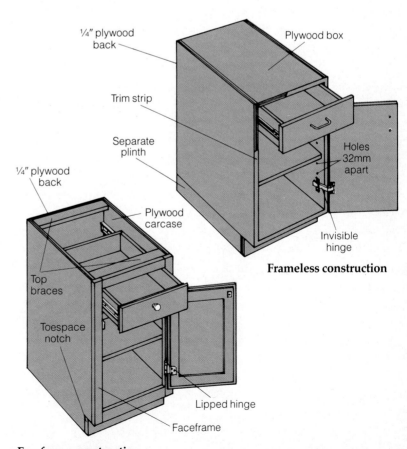

¼" plywood back

Trim strip

Separate plinth

Plywood box

Holes 32mm apart

Invisible hinge

Frameless construction

¼" plywood back

Plywood carcase

Top braces

Toespace notch

Lipped hinge

Faceframe

Faceframe construction

Stock, custom, or custom modular?

Cabinets are manufactured and sold in three different ways. The type you choose will affect the cost, overall appearance, and workability of your kitchen.

Stock cabinets. Buy your kitchen "off-the-shelf" and save—if you're careful. Mass-produced, standard-sized cabinets are the least expensive option, and they can be an excellent choice if you clearly understand the cabinetry you need for your kitchen. As the name implies, the range of sizes is limited.

Even so, you can always specify door styles, which direction they swing, and whether side panels are finished. And you can often get options and add-ons such as breadboards, sliding shelves, wine racks, and special corner units.

Most stock systems also have cabinets that can be ordered for peninsulas or islands, with doors or drawers on both sides and appropriate toespaces, trim, and finishes.

You may find stock lines heavily discounted at some home centers. But buying such cabinets can be a lot

COMPARING CABINETS

	Stock	Custom	Custom modular
Where to buy	Lumberyards, home improvement centers, appliance stores, some showrooms (most stock is made in this country).	Few shops have showrooms; most show pictures of completed jobs. Be safe; visit not only the shop but some installations, too.	If you know a brand name, check the yellow pages. These cabinets are mainly showroom items, but some are found in stock locations and department stores.
Who designs	You should, because the clerk helping you order may know less about cabinet options than you do. Don't order if you're at all unsure.	You; your architect, builder, or kitchen designer; or the maker (but be careful; cabinetmakers aren't necessarily designers).	The better (and more expensive) the line, the more help you get. Top-of-the-line suppliers design your whole kitchen; you just pick the style and write the check.
Cost range	Less than the other two choices, but you'll still swallow hard when you see the total. Look for heavy discounts at home centers, but pay attention to craftsmanship.	Very wide; depends, as with factory-made boxes, on materials, finishes, craftsmanship, and options you choose.	A basic box can cost about what stock does, but each desirable modification or upgrade in door and drawer finishes boosts the cost considerably.
Options available	Only options may be door styles, hardware, and door swing—but check the catalog; some lines offer a surprising range.	You can often—but not always—get the same options and European-made hardware that go in custom modular cabinets.	Most lines offer choices galore—including variations in basic sizes and options for corners. Check showrooms and study catalogs.
Materials used	Cheaper lines may use doors of mismatched or lower-quality woods, composite, or thinner laminates that photo-simulate wood.	Anything you specify, but see samples. Methods vary by cabinetmaker; look at door and drawer hardware in a finished kitchen.	Factory-applied laminates and catalyzed varnishes are usually high quality and durable. Medium-density fiberboard is superior alternative for nonshowing wood.
Delivery time	You may be able to pick up cabinets at a warehouse the same day you order. Wait is generally (but not always) shorter than other types.	Figure five weeks or longer, depending on job complexity, material and hardware availability, number of drawers, finishes.	Five to eight weeks is typical, whether cabinets are American or imported, but don't be surprised if they take up to six months. Order as soon as possible.
Installation & service	Depends on where you buy; supplier may recommend a contractor. Otherwise, you install yourself. Service is virtually nonexistent.	In most cases, the maker installs. Buy from an established shop and you should have no trouble getting service if something doesn't work right.	Better lines are sold at a price that includes installation and warranty (one of the reasons price is higher). Some cabinets are virtually guaranteed for life.
Other considerations	You often pay in full up front, giving you little recourse if cabinets are shipped wrong. Be sure order is absolutely correct and complete.	Make sure the bid you accept is complete—not just a basic cost-per-foot or cost-per-box charge.	With some manufacturers, if cabinets are wrong, you'll wait as long for the right parts to arrive as you did in the first place. Check.

Looking for a quick, economical kitchen makeover? Consider refacing. The old kitchen is shown above; refurbished cabinets at right have stained oak doors, drawer fronts, and facing panels set off by granite tile countertops.

like doing your own taxes: no one really volunteers much information that will save you money or clarify your options. If you make a mistake or someone (even a salesperson) gives you bad advice, you're still the one who's liable. Knowledgeable people who can help you select stock cabinets tend to be the exception, not the rule.

Custom cabinets. Many people still have a cabinetmaker come to their house and measure, then return to the cabinet shop and build custom frame carcases, drawers, and doors.

Custom cabinet shops can match old cabinets, size truly oddball configurations, and accommodate complexities that can't be handled with stock or modular cabinets. Such jobs generally cost considerably more than medium-line stock or modular cabinets.

Many cabinet shops take advantage of stock parts to streamline work and keep prices down. They buy door and drawer fronts from the same companies who make them for stock manufacturers. And cabinetmakers are using the same fine hardware (usually German) and tools (multiple-bit drills, metric hinge setters, and precise panel saws) developed for modular systems.

Some cabinet shops specialize in refacing existing kitchen cabinets. This can be an excellent, less expensive choice than replacing the entire cabinet system, with results that look essentially the same as if you had done just that.

Custom modular cabinets. Between stock and custom-made cabinetry are "custom modular cabinets" or "custom systems," which can offer the best of both worlds. They are manufactured, but they are of a higher grade and offer more design flexibility than stock cabinets. Not surprisingly, they cost more, too.

Custom systems offer a wide range of sizes, with many options within each size. A good modular shop can do all but true custom work, using its own components to build a kitchen from finished units. If necessary, heights, widths, and depths can be modified to fit almost any kitchen configuration.

You can change virtually everything on these basic modules: add sliding shelves; replace doors with drawers; set a matching hood unit over the stove; add wire baskets, flour bins, appliance garages, and pullout pantries.

Though frameless modular cabinets are sized metrically (standard depth is 60 centimeters—about 24 inches), nearly all lines are now sized for American appliances.

One thing agreed upon by modular retailers and custom shops alike is that frameless cabinets will replace faceframe ones as the dominant style. "At this point, faceframe is largely a look; it can be duplicated in frameless," one cabinetmaker told us.

Wall Cabinet Options

Wall cabinets come in singles, doubles, and various specialty configurations. Typically 12 or 15 inches deep, cabinets can vary in width from 9 to 60 inches. Although the most frequently used heights are 15, 18, and 30 inches, units range from 12 to 36 inches high, and even taller.

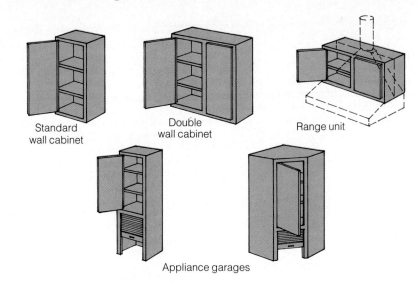

Standard wall cabinet

Double wall cabinet

Range unit

Appliance garages

What options are available?

The illustrations on these two pages show many of your basic cabinet choices; you'll find variations on these units in most cabinet lines.

Perhaps more options exist for corners than for any other kitchen cabinet space. The simplest corner butts one cabinet against another, providing inconvenient access to the corner. Better options include angled units with larger doors, double-door units that provide full access to the L-shaped space, and lazy Susans or other slide-out accessories that bring items from the back up to the front.

Hardware options are available to add to the versatility of kitchen cabinets. For examples, see page 69.

Judging quality

To determine the quality of a cabinet, look closely at the drawers; they take more of a beating than any other part of your cabinets. "Drawers are a cabinet within a cabinet," says one maker. "They tell all." Compare drawers in several lines, examining the joinery in each, and you'll begin to see differences.

Drawer guides and cabinet hinges are the critical hardware elements. Check for adjustability of both; they should be able to be reset and fine-tuned with the cabinets in place. Some frameless cabinets also have adjustable mounting hardware, so you can relevel them even after they're hanging on the wall.

Determine whether drawer guides allow full or only partial ex-

Base Cabinet Options

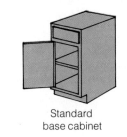

Standard base cabinet

Drawer unit

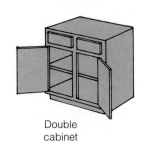

Double cabinet

When complete with a toespace or plinth, base cabinets normally measure 34½ inches tall; the counter adds another 1½ inches. In width, they range from 9 to 60 inches, increasing in increments of 3 inches from 9 to 36 inches and increments of 6 inches after that. Standard depth is 24 inches.

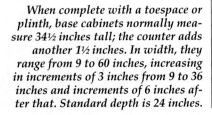

Pullout shelves

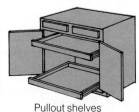

False sink front

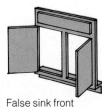

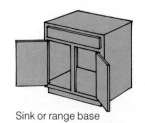

Sink or range base

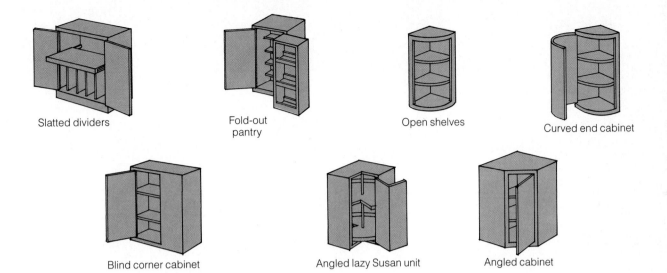

Slatted dividers

Fold-out pantry

Open shelves

Curved end cabinet

Blind corner cabinet

Angled lazy Susan unit

Angled cabinet

tension of drawers. Check to see that doors and drawers align properly.

Make sure laminate and edge banding are thick enough not to peel at the corners and edges. "Once they start peeling on a cheap cabinet, that's it," one shop warned.

Getting help

The cabinets are only part of the puzzle. When you buy cabinets, some of what you're paying for is varying degrees of help with the design.

A designer will help you figure out how you'll use the kitchen. Some retailers will give you a questionnaire (much like the one on page 9) to find out what's wrong with your current kitchen, how often you do any specialty cooking, whether your guests always end up in the kitchen, whether you buy food in bulk, and other helpful clues to the final design solution.

Pick a "look," then shop for it; compare features, craftsmanship, budget, and cost. Some designers

represent a particular line, so shop around to get an idea of what's currently available.

Your current floor plan (see page 8) is the best aid you can offer a designer. Some staff designers in showrooms will do the new cabinet plan for you, applying the charge against the purchase price of the cabinets. Some showrooms even use computer renderings to help customers visualize the finished kitchen—and prices for different cabinets are just a keystroke away.

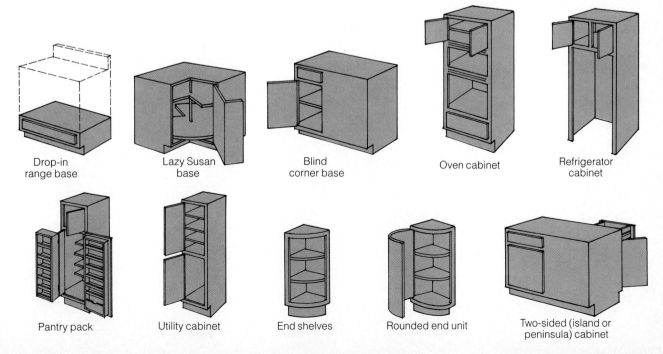

Drop-in range base

Lazy Susan base

Blind corner base

Oven cabinet

Refrigerator cabinet

Pantry pack

Utility cabinet

End shelves

Rounded end unit

Two-sided (island or peninsula) cabinet

Island cabinets utilize wasted floor space, define traffic patterns, and offer valuable preparation and storage space. A formal, handcarved island (above) divides the long corridor kitchen and augments cooking and cleanup centers. The freestanding table island (right) adds a furniture-like touch, providing movable counter space where it's needed.

CABINETS

And what will all this cost?

There are no figures after "Cost range" in the chart on page 64. Why? Because so many factors influence the final price. The kitchens you see on these pages have cabinets that range from about $400 to more than $80,000.

The wide range of styles—and prices—makes buying cabinets much like buying a car. Like car makers, every manufacturer or cabinetmaker picks a slot of the market, then offers various styles and options that raise or lower the basic price. If you're looking for the cabinet equivalent of "transportation," you can pay a lot less than someone looking for something sportier.

Know your budget. You'll quickly find out what kinds of cabinets you can afford; with your plan in hand, you can get a basic price for standard cabinets relatively easily. But options will drastically alter the quote—so the same basic cabinet can end up costing a lot of different prices. Bids should be full quotes based on a fully specified room sketch listing the options desired in each cabinet.

Within each line, basic costs are determined by the wood species and the style of the doors and drawers. Remember, the basic frame carcase will be the same within a line no matter what door style you choose.

Even if you're favoring manufactured cabinets, consider including a bid from a custom shop for comparison. As with stock and custom modular bids, make sure your plan is specific enough to get a reliable quote. Ask for complete shop drawings, so there's no misunderstanding as to what you're ordering.

An explosion of new hardware products awaits the cabinet shopper. Shown clockwise, from top right: swiveling spice rack; corner base lazy Susan; adjustable pullout shelf; sink unit with tilt-down front and specialty units; pantry pack's pivoting, pullout wire shelves.

COUNTERTOPS

Chop on it, knead on it, serve from it: you ask a lot, every day, of your kitchen countertop. No one material is best for all purposes, but each of the six described below looks distinctive and has specific advantages.

What are your choices?

Any one of these six surfaces can be installed throughout your kitchen.

But you might want to consider a combination, placing heat-resistant materials near the stove, easy-cleanup surfaces near the sink, a cool stone insert where it's handy for dough preparation.

The problem is that you probably won't find all the materials in the same place. Some dealers with showrooms are listed in the yellow pages under Kitchen Cabinets &

COMPARING COUNTERTOPS

DESIGNER: BERNADINE LEACH

Plastic laminate

Advantages. You can choose from a wide range of colors, textures, and patterns. Laminate is durable, easy to clean, water-resistant, and relatively inexpensive. With the right tools, you can install it yourself.

Disadvantages. It can scratch, scorch, chip, and stain, and it's hard to repair. Conventional laminate has a dark backing that shows at its seams; new solid-color laminates, designed to avoid this, are somewhat brittle and more expensive.

Cost. Standard brands cost $1 to $3.50 a square foot; premolded, particleboard-backed tops in limited colors are $5 to $10 per running foot. Installed, a custom countertop with 2-inch lip and low backsplash costs from $40 to $90 per running foot (more for solid-color materials).

Ceramic tile

Advantages. It's good-looking, comes in many colors, textures, and patterns, is heat-proof, scratch-resistant, and water-resistant if installed correctly. Grout is also available in numerous colors. Patient do-it-yourselfers are likely to have good results.

Disadvantages. Many people find it hard to keep grout satisfactorily clean. Some kitchen designers recommend using less grout space ($3/32$ inch versus the typical $1/4$ inch), but the thinner joint is definitely weaker. You can also buy grout sealers, but their effectiveness is disputed. Hard, irregular surface can chip china and glassware. High-gloss tiles show every smudge.

Cost. Prices range from 50 cents to $50 per square foot. Choose nonporous glazed tiles, which won't soak up spills and stains. Installation costs vary, depending on tile type and size of job (generally, the smaller the countertop, the higher the per-foot price).

DESIGNER: ESTHER H. REILLY

Solid-surface

Advantages. Durable, water-resistant, heat-resistant, nonporous, and easy to clean, this marble-like material can be shaped and installed with woodworking tools (but do it very carefully, or cracks can occur, particularly around cutouts). It allows for a variety of sink installations, including an integral unit like the one shown on page 74. Blemishes and scratches can be sanded out.

Disadvantages. It's expensive, and requires very firm support below. Until recently, color selection was limited to white, beige, and almond; now imitation stone and pastels are common.

Cost. For a 24-inch-deep counter with a 2-inch front lip and 4-inch backsplash, figure $100 to $150 per running foot, installed. Uninstalled it's about half that. Costs go up for wood inlays and other fancy edge details.

Equipment; they'll probably have tile, plastic laminate, solid-surface, and—maybe—wood. Larger building supply centers and lumberyards usually carry plastic laminate and wood. For the appropriate dealer or fabricator, check listings in the categories Marble—Natural, Plastics, Restaurant Equipment, Sheet Metal Work, and Tile. Kitchen designers, interior designers, and architects can also supply samples of countertop materials.

What experts say

The chefs, designers, and architects we spoke with did not agree on any single surface.

Chefs preferred stainless steel, granite, marble, or—if it could be kept sanitary—wood. Designers and architects agreed with them, to a point. Restaurant kitchens are decidedly different in three ways: they aren't designed to be aesthetically pleasing; they put far greater de-

mands on each work surface; and they're not usually places to economize, given the need for extreme durability.

Residential designers take a more realistic approach. Although homeowners might jump at the prospect of granite countertops, the cost is prohibitive for many. But, as one dealer told us, "You can combine materials to make a little piece of a really choice one go a long way—perhaps spend a lot on a small section of

---

COMPARING COUNTERTOPS

Wood

Advantages. Wood is handsome, natural, easily installed, and easy on glassware and china.

Disadvantages. It's harder to keep clean than nonporous materials. It can scorch and scratch, and it may blacken when near a source of moisture. You can seal it with mineral oil, but seal both sides or the counter may warp. It's a good idea to make an insert (or even the countertop itself) removable for easy cleaning or resurfacing. Or use a permanent protective sealer, such as polyurethane (but then you can't cut on it).

Cost. Maple butcher-block, the most popular, costs about $12 to $16 per square foot for 1½- to 1¾-inch thickness. Installed cost is $50 and up per running foot, including miters and cutouts. It's sold in 24-, 30-, and 36-inch widths. Smaller pieces are available for inserts. Oak, sugar pine, and birch are also used for counters.

Stainless steel

Advantages. Stainless steel is waterproof, heat-resistant, easy to clean, seamless, and durable. You can get a counter with a sink molded right in. It's great for a part of the kitchen where you'll be using water a lot.

Disadvantages. Don't cut on it, or you risk damaging both countertop and knife. Fabrication is expensive; you can, however, reduce the cost by using flat sheeting and a wood edge, as in the counter shown at right.

Cost. The price of 16-gauge stainless (about ¹⁄₁₆ inch thick) is about $5.50 per square foot, just for material. For sink cutouts, faucet holes, and bends and welds for edges and backsplashes, count on about 3 to 6 hours' fabrication time at about $45 per hour for an installed 6- to 10-foot-long counter. Custom detailing and high-chromium stainless up the price—as high as $300 to $500 per running foot.

Stone

Advantages: Granite and marble, both used for countertops, are beautiful natural materials. Their cool surface is very helpful when you're working with dough or making candy. They're heatproof, water-resistant, easy to clean, and very durable.

Disadvantages. Oil, alcohol, and any acid (such as those in lemons or wine) will stain marble or damage its high-gloss finish; granite can stand up to all of these. Solid slabs are very expensive; recently, some homeowners and designers have turned to stone tiles—including slate and limestone—as less expensive alternatives.

Cost. A custom-cut marble slab costs $40 to $70 per square foot, granite about $60 and up—polished and finished with a square or slightly beveled edge. Decorative edge details and the like add more. Marble counter inserts run $30 to $45 per square foot. Installation costs about $75 an hour.

Backsplashes, the areas above countertops or behind range or cooktop, are favorite spots for decoration. The wine-country kitchen below sports custom wine-label accent tiles above a solid-surface countertop. A Mexican kitchen's cooktop area (right) is a feast of handpainted tile.

DESIGNER: WALLY BRUESKE/DESIGN CABINET SHOWROOMS

ARCHITECT: SHAKESPEARE & BURNS

marble, but make up for it with a large section of less expensive laminate—and still get the benefits of both surfaces."

Backsplash fever

These days, countertops aren't the only area where designers are making a fashion statement; the backsplash—the wall surface between the countertop proper and the wall cabinets overhead—is now artistically in vogue as well. (This area usually stretches for about 18 vertical inches—from 36 to about 54 inches from the floor.) The wall behind a freestanding range or cooktop is another model for design; there's usually more room there for a special statement. A good backsplash also has a practical side: if properly installed, it seals this vulnerable area from moisture penetration, and it makes the wall a lot easier to keep clean.

Just a few years ago, the average countertop, usually laminate, included a 4-inch lip on the back. Today's higher backsplashes, however, often feature materials that are found there alone. Geometric tile patterns and handpainted accent tiles are favorite choices. Stone tiles are an economical alternative to solid granite or marble (for visual spark, try laying these 8- or 12-inch squares on the diagonal). Even stainless steel and mirrored surfaces are showing up in high-tech surroundings. Under-cabinet strip lights (see pages 91–93) can add drama, too.

Need more inspiration? The photos in Chapter 2 present a wide variety of backsplash treatments.

SINKS & FITTINGS

The cleanup center is the number one command post of nearly every busy kitchen; in fact, studies claim that up to 50 percent of kitchen time is spent there. So doesn't it make sense to pay special attention to sinks, faucets, and related accessories when you're planning your new kitchen?

Recently, sinks and faucets have become prime design accents—an imaginative way to add a splash of color to an otherwise restrained design scheme. And if you later decide you don't like the boldness, it's a lot easier to change a sink or faucet than your kitchen cabinets!

The new world of sinks

When it comes to main kitchen sinks, the single-bowl version is mostly a thing of the past. Today's sink is a multitask center, and double-, even triple-bowl designs are now the norm. They come detailed with many custom-fitted accessories, such as cutting boards, colanders, rinsing baskets, and dish racks.

Sink color is a new realm, too: white and stainless are still tops, but red, black, and a rainbow of other designer tones are on the scene, too. Colored bowl strainers and accessories are also available.

Materials. Common sink materials include stainless steel, enameled cast iron or steel, vitreous china, brass, and copper.

■ *Stainless steel.* Stainless steel sinks come in 18- or 20-gauge (18-gauge is stronger) and either matte or mirror finish. Chromium/nickel blends—such as Type 302 stainless—are tops. These are the only true "stainless" sinks; cheaper grades will stain. Matte finishes are much easier to keep looking clean than mirrored, and they mask scratches better.

Stainless is relatively noisy; look for a sink with an undercoating. Integral drain boards are available, too.

■ *Enameled cast iron/steel.* Here's where the colors come in. These sinks are gaining in popularity, especially with the advent of new European designs. Black, gray, and a palette of other colors and flecked patterns are available. Enameled cast-iron sinks have a heavier layer of baked-on enamel than steel, making them quieter and less likely to chip, but also more expensive.

■ *Quartz.* A new, expensive import from Europe, quartz sinks look similar to enamel but stand abuse better and are easier to clean.

■ *Vitreous china.* Vitreous china sinks, a common bathroom component, are starting to show up in the kitchen. These are highly ornamental, sculpted sinks but very expensive.

■ *Integral solid-surface sinks.* Today's solid-surface countertops (see page 70) can be coupled with a molded, integral sink for a sleek, sculpted look. Sink color can either

ARCHITECT: J. ALLEN SAYLES

Sinks are more stylish and functional than ever. Sleek vitreous china sink (top right) is a newcomer, features strainer and chopping board inserts; stainless steel models, such as triple-bowl model with dish rack and strainer (bottom right), are still most popular. Bar sink (top) shows off its bright brass punch.

match the countertop exactly or complement it—for example, you might choose a cream-colored sink below a granite-colored top. Edge-banding and other border options abound. Although they're not indestructible, solid-surface sinks can be repaired if nicked or scratched.

■ *Brass and copper sinks.* These strikingly elegant surfaces are outstanding as accents. However, they require zealous maintenance, so you'll probably want to reserve them for wet-bar or other occasional uses. Bar or hospitality sinks come with either a 2- or 3½-inch drain opening; if you're planning to add a disposer you'll want the larger opening.

Rim or no rim? You also have a choice of mounting methods with various sink models. *Self-rimming* sinks with molded overlaps are supported by the edge of the countertop cutout; *flush* deck-mounted sinks have surrounding metal strips to hold the basin to the countertop; *unrimmed* sinks are recessed under the countertop and held in place by metal clips.

Faucets

Today's kitchen faucets fall into one of two camps: Euro-sophistication or traditional. Enameled single-lever fixtures with pullout sprayers and in-

How about a seamless, solid-surface sink? The one above is white-on-white, with decorative grooving and adjacent drainboard; other models have contrasting sink colors or border designs.

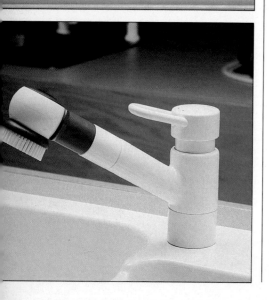

Like sinks, faucets are now design accents—they come in a rainbow of choices. The traditional brass gooseneck model (top left) is popular for country kitchens; single-lever European styles (middle and bottom left) offer bright colors, interchangeble attachments, and pullout sprayers.

terchangeable attachments are fashionable, but traditional brass or chrome gooseneck styles with individual handles remain popular, too. Whatever you choose, most kitchen professionals agree that solid-brass construction is the way to go.

When you select your sink, be sure the holes in it will accommodate the type of faucet you plan to buy as well as any additional accessories.

Garbage disposers

Today's garbage disposers handle almost all types of food waste. They come in two types: batch-feed and continuous. Batch-feed disposers kick into gear when you engage the lid; continuous-feed models are activated by an adjacent wall switch.

Look for sturdy motors (½ horsepower or more), noise insulation, and antijam features. Generally, the fatter the disposer, the more the insulation—and the quieter it's likely to run.

Hot & cold water dispensers

Half-gallon-capacity instant hot water dispensers have been around for some time now. The heater fits underneath the sink (see drawing below); connected to the cold water supply, it delivers 190° to 200°F water. Most units plug into a 120-volt grounded outlet installed inside the sink cabinet. Mount the dispenser spout either on a sink knockout or nearby on the countertop.

Cold water spouts operate in a similar manner, but a below-counter chiller is substituted for the heater.

Water purifiers

New compact water purifiers look just like hot water or soap dispensers on the sink; the main unit fits compactly underneath the sink like other water appliances. Look for a government approval seal and easy-to-change filter cartridges.

Hot-water dispenser, providing 190° to 200F° water on demand, is a common inhabitant of modern kitchens. Mount the spout on the sink on adjacent countertop; the tank resides below-deck.

The drawing at right shows the mysterious underworld of today's kitchen sink, where fittings and pipes abound. Dishwasher and garbage disposer link with the sink drain; both the dishwasher and hot water dispenser tap into supply lines on the way to the faucet. Electrical connections may be either plug-in or hard-wired; be sure your circuit capacity is up to local codes.

Inside the Sink Complex

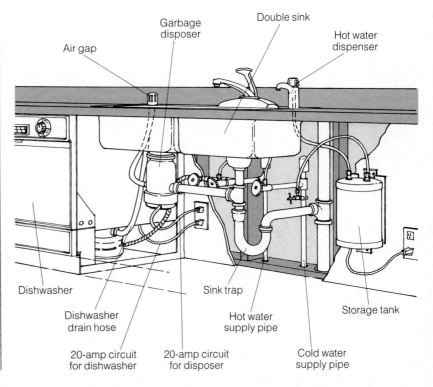

Air gap

Garbage disposer

Double sink

Hot water dispenser

Dishwasher

Dishwasher drain hose

20-amp circuit for dishwasher

20-amp circuit for disposer

Sink trap

Hot water supply pipe

Cold water supply pipe

Storage tank

Ranges

What's best, the flexibility of separate cooktops and ovens or the traditional integrated range? On one level, the choice is one of function. But in addition to that, it's a question of style: the range creates a focal point, invoking the traditional image of "hearth and home."

Freestanding, slide-in, or drop-in?

Take your choice of three types of ranges: freestanding, slide-in (freestanding without side panels to fit between cabinets), and drop-in. Most ranges have a cooktop with oven below; a few models offer an additional upper microwave oven with a built-in ventilator or downventing cooktop. Standard range width is 30 inches, but sizes go as narrow as 21 inches and, in commercial designs, as wide as 48 inches or more.

Which style is for you?

Choose from standard models—gas or electric, commercial units, or new residential/commercial. For a discussion of burner options, see pages 78–79; for oven specifics, turn to pages 80–81.

■ *Electric ranges* may have standard coils, solid-element burners, or a smooth ceramic top, plus radiant-heat or convection/radiant ovens.

Today's freestanding range is often the kitchen's focal point, set off by a backsplash, vent hood, or shiny pots and pans. The residential/commercial range (facing page) has custom enamel finish; here it's coupled with a brass hood and granite tile backsplash. The Southwest design at right fits range, pots, spices, and exhaust fan into a homey tiled alcove.

■ *Gas ranges* have either radiant-heat or convection ovens; lower ovens may be self-cleaning or continuous-cleaning. Some models offer interchangeable modules.

■ *Commercial gas units* have been a "hot" item in recent years—partly due to increased BTU output, partly because of their look of "serious business." Their performance is excellent, but they create many problems for home use: they're not as well insulated as residential units; they may be too heavy for your floor; they're tough to clean; and they're potentially dangerous for young children.

■ *Residential/commercial units,* a recent response to the commercial craze, were designed specifically for the home. These have the commercial look and the high BTU output but are better insulated; they also offer additional niceties such as self- or continuous-cleaning ovens.

DESIGNER: JERRI GOLDEN

COOKTOPS

For extra flexibility, specialized needs, or simply a trim, modern look, separate cooktops make good sense. The explosive use of island and peninsula designs supports this trend.

A conventional gas or electric cooktop is built into a counter like a sink, with connections below. Unless you buy a downventing model, the unit will require an overhead hood (for more on venting, see pages 82–83). Typical units have four burners, though some have five, six, or even more.

Standard cooktop finishes include stainless steel, enameled cast iron or steel, and glass—either black or white. Sizes range from 15 to 48 inches wide, 18 to 25 inches deep, and 3 to 8 inches high (16½ inches high for downventing models).

Convertible gas or electric cooktops are similar to conventional models but offer interchangeable and reversible modules that let you replace burners with a grill, a griddle, and other specialty items.

Commercial or residential/commercial (see page 77) gas units house up to eight burners; many styles combine hot plates or griddles. Typically, these are 6 to 7 inches high with short legs for installing on a base of tile, brick, or other noncombustible material.

COMPARING COOKTOPS

Smoothtop (ceramic glass)

Electric smoothtop cooktops have burners similar to traditional coil designs but with ceramic glass on top, which disperses heat and makes the cooktop much easier to clean. In the past, these tops have received thumbs down for slow heating, but newer designs have coils closer to the surface; some models also include fast-starting coils. These units have also been slow to cool, but warning lights on some new models stay on until the top is safe to touch.

Early smoothtops also scratched or cracked, but newer formulations are more durable. Popular finishes include classic black and flecked patterns (which hide abrasions). Typically, units have three to four burners; look for independent sizing controls for smaller or larger pans. You also might be able to combine burners—to handle a large poacher, for example.

Smoothtop surfaces require flat-bottom pans for best heat dispersal.

Solid-element electric

Wander into any showroom with imported cooktops and you'll see these trim-looking burner units. They're basically cast-iron disks with resistance coils below. Because of the continuous surface, the disks produce more even heat than standard coils; and because they're sealed, they're also easier to clean.

These elements are housed in either a standard four-burner conventional top or in modules with two or three burners of different sizes. With some models, central "button" sections glow when the power is on. Better models have thermostats or on-off cycles to keep heat even and protect the unit.

Owner complaints? Solid-element burners may not produce enough heat for certain types of cooking. They also remain hot to the touch for a long time after the unit is turned off. The disks may discolor over time or with overzealous scrubbing.

Like smoothtop surfaces (discussed above), solid-element disks require flat-bottomed pans for best results.

Mix-and-match cooktop modules (often called "hobs") are the newest thing, and they're showing up everywhere. Modules, typically 12 inches wide, may be grouped together with connecting hardware or embedded separately, if you choose. Modules include standard gas, high-BTU-output gas, halogen, smoothtop electric, solid-element electric, barbecue, griddle, electric wok, or deep fryer (which some cooks use as a steamer). Some of these units fit in as little as 2 inches of vertical space, freeing up the cabinet below for drawers or a complementary oven.

Modular cooktop systems allow the cook to "mix and match" individual units; modules may be grouped together or placed individually. Shown above, from left to right, are gas, electric smoothtop, and grill units.

COMPARING COOKTOPS

Halogen

The latest technological kitchen marvel, halogen, seems the heir apparent to magnetic induction as the cutting edge of heat sources. Still more expensive to operate than gas, halogen is nonetheless the most efficient electric source; and, unlike most electric burners, halogen offers rapid on-off and infinite adjustment controls.

Halogen burners come as one of a pair of burners in 12-inch modules, or in standard four-burner set-ups combining one halogen with three standard smoothtop burners. Like other smoothtop units, many halogen cooktops now come with warning lights that stay on until the burner has completely cooled.

Halogen's weakness? It's still quite expensive—$800 to $900 per unit. The light can burn out, but it is expected to last approximately eight years before needing replacement.

Gas

Gas cooktops are the choice of most gourmet cooks; they respond instantly when turned on or off, or when settings are changed. Gas is also more economical to operate than any electric alternative.

Typical gas cooktops are 30 to 36 inches wide and feature four, five, or even six burners. Smaller modular units house two standard burners, or one standard (8,000 BTU) and one "commercial" (12,000 BTU or hotter). Pilotless ignition eliminates pilot lights, saves gas (up to 30 percent), but requires an electrical hookup.

Drawbacks? Some people find that gas smells; it may be harder to maintain than an electrical heat source. Commercial gas units may require special installation as well as heavy-duty cookware to stand up to high temperatures. Simmering can be difficult.

OVENS

Built-in ovens save counter space by hiding inside base cabinets or special vertical storage units. In separate ovens, as in cooktops, you have several choices: conventional gas or electric, microwave, and convection.

Combining a conventional radiant-heat oven with a microwave or energy-saving convection oven is a popular choice. Double ovens can be installed one above the other (with controls at eye level), or side by side below the countertop (some find this a clever use of space, others totally inefficient). You can also install a "built-under" combination unit directly below the cooktop of your choice. Your oven's interior may be "easy-off" (old-fashioned elbow grease required), continuous (a steady, slow process), or self-cleaning (the most effective method).

Radiant-heat ovens

Conventional radiant-heat ovens are available in single or double units. Single ovens range from 25 to 32 inches high and 23 to 28½ inches deep (you'll probably need extra depth for venting). The most common width is 27 inches, though many

DESIGNER: JULIE ATWOOD DESIGN

Double wall ovens (left) deliver multiple cooking options and slide neatly into an end-of-run oven cabinet; they're flanked by matching warming trays. A built-under oven (above) provides a range effect without interrupting countertop; add the cooktop of your choice.

Locate a microwave where you'll use it most: in the cooking center; near the refrigerator; or, as shown at top right, adjacent to a break- fast counter. The same rule goes for small built-ins; the toaster shown below right pops out of the back- splash area.

"space-efficient" European imports are 24 inches; recently, the 30-inch oven has also caught on. Even one 36-inch unit is available.

You can choose to include built-in warmer shelves, rotisseries, attached meat thermometers, variable-speed broilers, multiple-rack systems, pizza inserts, digital clock and timing devices, and decorator colors.

Microwave ovens

Foods cook quickly with high-frequency microwaves, but they seldom brown. Some models offer a separate browning element; other units combine microwave with radiant and/or convection cooking. Sizes range from 13 to 17 inches high, 22 to 27 inches wide, and 17 to 22 inches deep. Most units are hinged on the left.

Microwaves can be placed on a counter, built into cabinetry, or purchased as part of a double wall oven or double oven range. Some models, specially designed to be installed above a range (underneath wall cabinets), incorporate a vent and cooking lights; these are wider (30 inches) and shallower (13 to 17 inches deep). Some designers frown on the over-the-cooktop placement because it's potentially hazardous. You might even consider two microwaves—one small, portable unit near the refrigerator for quick cooking, the second in a bank of wall ovens.

Features include memory bank, programmable cooking, timers, temperature probe, rotisserie, and electronic sensors (these automatically calculate cooking time and power levels).

Convection ovens

Gas or electric convection ovens circulate hot air around the oven cavity. (You can tell them by the fan.) More energy-efficient than radiant-heat ovens, they cut cooking time by 30 percent and use reduced temperatures.

Unlike those from the microwave oven, convection-cooked foods do brown, and nicely at that. Convection is excellent for roasting and baking (it first caught on in commercial bakeries) but is less effective for foods cooked in deep or covered dishes (cakes, stews, casseroles).

Convection units vary from microwave size to standard radiant-heat size.

VENTILATION

Your main choice is between a hood (freestanding, wall-attached, or cabinet-mounted) and a downdraft system. A ceiling fan, although not strictly a venting option, can be a useful, stylish addition.

Installing a kitchen without planning for proper ventilation is akin to lighting a fire in the fireplace without opening the flue. The system you choose must tackle smoke, heat, grease, moisture, and odors, while remaining as quiet as possible (8 sones or less). Vent units range from totally discreet to bold and flashy.

Vent hoods

Unless your range is downvented, you'll need a hood over the cooktop. Ducted hoods channel air outside; roof- or wall-mounted exterior blowers are the best blend of quiet operation and efficiency. If exterior venting is impossible, ductless hoods draw out some smoke and grease through charcoal filters.

A hood should cover the entire cooking area and extend 3 to 6 inches on each side; place its bottom edge 21 to 30 inches above the cooking surface. Commercial ranges (see page 77) and cooktops really crank out the heat: you'll need to make extra provisions for these.

Downdraft systems

If your kitchen style is open and orderly, you may wish to substitute a downdraft system in the range or

DESIGNER: BERNADINE LEACH/KITCHENS BY DESIGN

A vent hood not only provides an exit route for smoke, heat, and grease: it can look great, too. This elegant stainless unit matches edgings on both main and island countertops, as well as decorative moldings at the ceiling line.

A trim overhead vent shield (bottom left) pulls out to catch heat and grease, slides back when not in use. Cooktop downdraft system (bottom right) is discreet, great for islands and peninsulas. Although not strictly a venting option, a ceiling fan (top) helps circulate air and makes a design statement, too.

cooktop—especially if the unit is housed in an island or peninsula. Standard, convertible, and modular cooktops all come with downventing options. Some have grillwork between cooktop modules or units; others run along the back (more common with ranges). The downdraft unit sets up air currents that draw smoke, heat, and moisture down; grease is trapped below.

Are there drawbacks? Downvents don't work as well on a tall stockpot as on a skillet at cooktop level. There have been problems with long, twisted duct runs, but recent systems are more efficient than those available just a few years ago. Always route a downdraft system to the closest outside wall (see the drawing at right).

What size do you need?

The power of a fan or blower is rated in cubic feet per minute (CFM). To find the minimum acceptable number of CFM for your space, the formula is:

cubic feet x 15 ÷ 60

Figure cubic feet by multiplying width times length times height (in feet). Multiply this figure by 15, the minimum recommendation for air exchanges per hour. Then divide by 60 (minutes) to get the *minimum* acceptable CFM rating for your hood. If your cooking center is on an island or peninsula, multiply the result again by 1½ times.

Two overhead options for routing duct from a vent hood: take the direct route up through the cabinet, ceiling, and attic (A); or run it horizontally over wall cabinets in a soffit (B). Downventing is another choice: run the duct through base cabinets or below the floor (C).

Three Paths for a Vent Duct

A) To roof

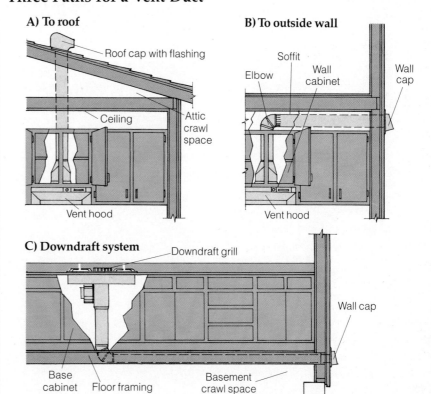

Roof cap with flashing

Ceiling

Attic crawl space

Vent hood

B) To outside wall

Soffit

Elbow

Wall cabinet

Wall cap

Vent hood

C) Downdraft system

Downdraft grill

Wall cap

Base cabinet

Floor framing

Basement crawl space

REFRIGERATORS

Refrigerators come in three basic versions: freestanding, built-in, and undercounter. Standard refrigerators measure from 27 to 32 inches deep, so they stand out from 24-inch-deep base cabinets. Gaining popularity are the relatively expensive 24-inch "built-ins;" most models offer interchangeable door panels to blend better with a cabinet run.

Consider these features: number of shelves, humidity drawers, meat storage compartments, temperature controls, defrosting method, icemaker and water dispenser, convenience door, and energy-saving devices such as a power-saver switch.

Popular two- or three-door, side-by-side refrigerators permit easy visibility and access to food, but their relatively narrow shelves make it difficult to store bulky items. Other two-door models have the freezer positioned at the unit's top or bottom; the bottom mount makes it easier to reach the more often-used refrigerator sections.

Eight cubic feet of refrigerator space is recommended for two people; add a cubic foot for each additional family member and 2 extra feet if you entertain frequently. Two cubic feet per person is the rule for a freezer compartment. Typical capacities are 18.7 to 27.6 cubic feet for side-by-side refrigerators; 12 to 32 cubic feet for top-mount models; and 16.2 to 22 feet for bottom-mounts.

Undercounter refrigerators, handy for a specialty cooking center or separate entertainment area, are 33 to 34 inches high, 18 to 57 inches wide, and 25 to 32 inches deep, with a 2.5- to 6-cubic foot capacity.

DESIGNER; JULIE ATWOOD DESIGN

Organization is the byword in refrigerators. At left, faux painting, stenciling, and wrap-around niches add country charm to a glass-doored, commercial refrigerator. The view inside the built-in unit above shows a well-orchestrated system of shelves, bins, and racks. Be sure, when choosing, that you can store bulky items as needed.

DISHWASHERS & TRASH COMPACTORS

More often than not, today's cleanup centers include both a dishwasher and trash compactor—one on either side of the main sink. Here are some shopping tips.

Dishwashers

Whether portable or built-in, most dishwashers are standard size: roughly 24 inches wide, 24 inches deep, and 34 inches high. One manufacturer offers a compact 18-inch-wide built-in or portable unit; another has an undersink model for small spaces. Standard finishes include enameled steel (usually white, black, or almond), black glass, or replaceable panels to match base cabinet runs.

Quiet is the name of the game in dishwashers: improved insulation has led to operating levels as low as 50 dB. Look for such energy-saving devices as a booster heater that raises the water temperature for the dishwasher only, separate cycles for lightly or heavily soiled dishes, and air-drying options. Other features include a delay start that allows you to wash dishes at a preset time (during the night instead of at peak-energy hours), prerinse and potscrubbing cycles, a strainer filtering system (actually like a small disposer), and adjustable and/or removable racks.

Trash compactors

Compactors reduce bulky trash such as cartons, cans, and bottles to a fourth of the original size. A normal compacted load—a week's worth of trash from a family of four—will weigh 20 to 28 pounds.

Features include reversible manual or automatic doors, a separate top-bin door for loading small items (even while the unit is operating), drop-down or tilt-out drawers for easy bag removal, and a charcoal-activated filter or deodorizer to control odor. Also look for such features as a toe-operated door latch and key-activated safety switch. Sizes vary from 12 to 18 inches wide (15 inches is standard), 18 to 24½ inches deep, and 34 to 36 inches high.

Remember that a compactor is for dry, clean trash only—you'll still have to do some sorting.

The ultraquiet dishwasher at right has three tiers of rack space, including a removable flatware tray. A typical cleanup center is shown below: dishwasher and trash compactor flank main sink, facing panels blend with surrounding cabinets.

ARCHITECT: WILLIAM B. REMICK

FLOORING

Two primary requirements for a kitchen floor are moisture resistance and durability. Resilient sheet flooring, ceramic tile, and properly sealed masonry or hardwood all make good candidates. Resilient flooring is the simplest (and usually the least expensive) of the four to install; the other three are trickier. And don't rule out carpeting, especially newer stain-resistant, industrial versions.

Planning checkpoints

Confused by the array of flooring types available today? For help, study the guide below. Also, it's a good idea to visit flooring suppliers and home improvement centers; most dealers are happy to provide samples.

Beyond aesthetic considerations, you should weigh the physical char-

---

COMPARING FLOORING

Resilient

Advantages. Generally made from solid vinyl, rubber (shown at right), or polyurethane, resilients are flexible, moisture- and stain-resistant, easy to install, and simple to maintain. Another advantage is the seemingly endless variety of colors, textures, patterns, and styles available. Tiles can be mixed to form custom patterns or provide color accents.

Sheets run up to 12 feet wide, eliminating the need for seaming in some kitchens; tiles are generally 12 inches square. Vinyl and rubber are comfortable to walk on. Polyurethane finish eliminates the need for waxing.

Disadvantages. Resilients are relatively soft, making them vulnerable to dents and tears; often, though, such damage can be repaired. Tiles may collect moisture between seams if improperly installed. Some vinyl still comes with a photographically applied pattern, but most is inlaid; the latter is more expensive but wears much better.

Cost. Vinyl is least expensive. It's a good do-it-yourself project if your kitchen shape is simple; tiles are often easier to lay than sheet goods.

DESIGNER: PLUS KITCHENS

Ceramic tile

Advantages. Made from hard-fired slabs of clay, ceramic tile is available in dozens of patterns, colors, shapes, and finishes. Its durability, easy upkeep, and attractiveness are definite advantages.

Tiles are usually classified as *quarry tile,* commonly unglazed (unfinished) red-clay tiles that are rough and water-resistant; *pavers,* rugged unglazed tiles in earthtone shades; and *glazed tile,* available in glossy, matte, or textured finishes and in many colors.

Tile sizes run the gamut of widths, lengths, and thicknesses: by mixing sizes and colors, creative tile workers can fashion a wide range of border treatments and field accents.

Disadvantages. Tile can be cold, noisy, and, if glazed, slippery underfoot. If not properly grouted, tiles can leak moisture; some tiles will stain unless properly sealed. Grout spaces can be tough to keep clean.

Cost. Tile can cost from about $1 per square foot to nearly $40, uninstalled. Those with three-dimensional patterns and multicolored glazes can easily double costs. Purer clays fired at higher temperatures generally make costlier but better wearing tiles.

ARCHITECT: WILLIAM B. REMICK

acteristics of flooring materials. Kitchen floors take a lot of wear and tear. Is your choice water-resistant, durable, and easy to maintain? Is it hard to walk on, noisy, or slippery underfoot?

What about subflooring?

Don't make any final flooring decision until you know the kind and condition of the subfloor your new flooring will cover.

With proper preparation, a concrete slab can serve as a base for almost any type of flooring. Other subfloors are more flexible and not suitable for rigid materials such as masonry and ceramic tile unless they are built up with extra underlayment or floor framing. Too many layers underneath can make the kitchen floor awkwardly higher than surrounding rooms. Be sure to check with a building professional or a flooring dealer for specifics.

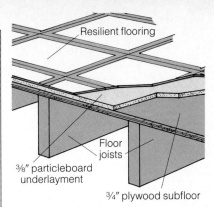

Resilient flooring

Floor joists

⅜" particleboard underlayment

¾" plywood subfloor

Solid, smooth support is crucial to a successful flooring job.

COMPARING FLOORING

Hardwood

Advantages. A classic hardwood floor creates a warm decor, feels good underfoot, resists wear, and can be refinished. Oak is most common; maple, birch, and beech are also available.

The three basic types are *strip*, narrow tongue-and-groove boards in random lengths; *plank*, tongue-and-groove boards in various widths and random lengths; and *wood tile*, often laid in blocks or squares, often in parquet fashion. "Floating" floor systems (one is shown at right) have several veneered strips atop each tongue-and-groove backing board. Wood flooring may be factory-prefinished or unfinished, so that it can be sanded and finished in place. Most floors can be refinished; floating systems cannot.

Disadvantages. Moisture damage and inadequate floor substructure are two bugaboos. Maintenance is another issue: some surfaces can be mopped, some cannot. Bleaching and some staining processes may wear unevenly and are difficult to repair.

Cost. From $7.50 to $13 per square foot, installed, depending on type, quality, and finish. Floating systems are generally most expensive.

Stone

Advantages. Natural stone, such as slate, flagstone, marble, granite, and limestone, has been used as flooring for centuries. Today, its use is even more practical, thanks to the development of sealers and finishes. Easy to maintain, masonry flooring is also virtually indestructible.

Stone can be used in its natural shape or cut into uniform pieces—rectangular blocks or more formal tiles. Generally, uniform pieces are butted tightly together; irregular flagstone requires grouted joints.

Man-made masonry products, specifically heat-retaining brick, are also an option for indoor use. Even colored or textured concrete can be used for finish flooring.

Disadvantages. The cost of most masonry flooring is high. Moreover, the weight of the materials requires a very strong, well-supported subfloor. Some stone—marble in particular—is cold and slippery underfoot. Careful sealing is a must; certain stones, such as limestone or granite, absorb stains and dirt readily.

Cost. From $3 per square foot for slate to $30 and over for granite.

WALLS & CEILINGS

Adrift in the happy haze of choosing cabinets and appliances, many homeowners forget to plan for wall and ceiling treatments. Yet these surfaces go a long way toward defining the overall impact of your kitchen. Below, we'll take a brief look at your options.

Wall coverings

In addition to the backsplash areas (see page 72), your kitchen will probably include a good bit of wall space. Here are seven popular treatments.

Paint. Of course, everybody thinks of paint first, but what's best for the kitchen? Your basic choices are latex and alkyd paint.

Latex is easy to work with, and best of all, you can clean up wet paint with soap and water. Alkyd paint (often called oil-base paint) provides high gloss and will hang on a little harder than latex; however, alkyds are harder to apply and require cleanup with mineral spirits.

In general, high resin content is the mark of durable, abrasion-resistant, flexible paint—the kind you need in a kitchen. Usually, the higher the resin content the higher the gloss, so look for products labeled *gloss* or *semi-gloss* if you want a tough, washable finish.

An excellent choice for kitchen cabinets and woodwork is interior/exterior, quick-drying alkyd enamel;

it has a brilliant, tilelike finish that's extremely durable.

Stenciling. Stenciling, a traditional form of wall decoration, is regaining some of its former popularity, even as it takes on some modern interpretations. You can pick up a pattern or the colors from draperies, upholstery, or ceramic tiles, or you can create your own design.

Faux finishing. Faux (or, literally speaking, *false*) finishes produce in paint the appearance of other patterns or textures.

In one version, many closely related pastels are built up in subtle layers with brush strokes, by stippling, or with a sponge. Other faux finishes are bolder—including layers of textured paint and/or contrasting colors to mimic anything from traditional wallpaper to modern art.

Wallpaper. A wallpaper for the kitchen should be scrubbable, durable, and stain resistant. Solid vinyl wallpapers, available in a wide variety of colors and textures, fill the bill.

Plaster. The textured, uneven, and slightly rounded edges of plaster give a kitchen a custom, informal feel; plaster is especially popular for Southwest theme kitchens. The only

Faux-finished walls and ceiling (facing page), plus wall and floor stenciling, help integrate a 1937-vintage range with modern granite and pendant lights. The remodeled kitchen at right is linked to great-room addition via exposed beams and pitched ceiling; skylight and soffit uplighting help brighten things up.

drawback: The surface, if too irregular, is hard to keep clean.

Wood. Tongue-and-groove wood paneling—natural, stained, bleached, or painted—provides a charming accent to country design schemes. Wainscoting is most popular, sepa-rated from wallpaper or paint above by the traditional chair rail.

Glass block. If you're looking for some ambient daylight but don't want to lose your privacy to a window, consider another oldtimer—glass block. These masonry units produce a soft, filtered light that complements many kitchen designs.

DESIGNER: DAVID SKOMSVOLD

Blue-and-white pinstriped wallpaper (above) adds subtle accent to kitchen's end wall and open soffits. Plastered soffit shelves (left) are home to colorful turtles and other Mexican collectibles.

DESIGNER: DAVID SKOMSVOLD

Ceiling treatments

Don't worry—you needn't be stuck with that old acoustic ceiling or fluorescent panel. Here's a brief survey of your alternatives.

Open it up. If your one-story house has an attic or crawl space above, you may be able to remove ceiling joists—or add more widely spaced beams—and forgo the ceiling material. Track lights and hanging pendants are popular accompaniments. You'll need to finish off the underside of the roof decking, either with tongue-and-groove wood planks or with drywall and paint. And, of course, this is the perfect time to add a skylight for extra light.

Add hollow beams. Certain kitchen styles—for example, French country—incorporate patterned beams and enclosed ceiling bays (usually painted drywall). The hollow beams are built up from 2-by lumber and molding, and provide a bonus: the inner raceways are efficient spots to hide electrical and plumbing lines or heating ducts.

Lower it. A bumpy or worn-out surface, glaring ceiling panels, or a too-tall space can all be remedied in one of two ways. Where there is no framework, first install horizontal ceiling joists; then apply a new drywall ceiling and finish it as you wish. Or nail 1-by "furring strips" over an existing ceiling, then add drywall as before.

Size up the soffits. Remember that you have several choices in the soffit space between wall cabinets and ceiling. An open soffit makes a nice display nook or can house uplighting to "lift" a ceiling. Or you might emphasize vertical lines by filling the space with taller-than-average wall cabinets. Or enclose the area with drywall or molded plaster, perhaps extending the soffits past the cabinet fronts and adding recessed downlights (see pages 91–93).

LIGHT FIXTURES

Today's designers separate lighting into three categories: task, ambient, and accent. Task lighting illuminates a particular area where a visual activity—such as slicing stir-fry vegetables—takes place. Ambient, or general, lighting fills in the undefined areas of a room with a soft level of light—enough, say, to munch a midnight snack by. Primarily decorative, accent lighting is used to highlight architectural features, to set a mood, or to provide drama.

What fixtures are best?

Generally speaking, *small* and *discreet* are the bywords in kitchen light fixtures; consequently, recessed downlights are by far the most popular choice in today's kitchens. Fitted with the right baffle or shield, these fixtures alone can handle ambient, task, and accent needs. Typically, downlights follow countertops or shine on the sink or island. Track lights or mono-spots also offer pinpoint task lighting or can be aimed at a wall to provide a wash of ambient light.

In addition, designers frequently tuck task lighting behind a valance under wall cabinets and over countertops. And just for fun, why not consider decorative strip lights in the kickspace area or soffit?

Surface-mounted fixtures, once a kitchen mainstay, are now used specifically to draw attention. Hanging pendants are especially popular:

While downlights are number one in kitchens, these three fixture types are also popular. A track fixture (upper left) shines down from ceiling soffit; an undercabinet strip (upper right) lights up the countertop; decorative pendants (right) illuminate the island and dining area.

place them over a breakfast nook or an island—or anywhere else they won't present a hazard.

Dimmers (also called rheostats) enable you to set a fixture or group of fixtures at any level from a soft glow to a radiant brightness. They're also energy savers.

DESIGNER: OSBURN DESIGN

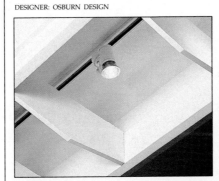

DESIGNER: KITCHENS BY STEWART

Light bulbs & tubes

Light sources can be grouped in general categories according to the way they produce light.

Incandescent light. This light, the kind used most frequently in our homes, is produced by a tungsten

thread that burns slowly inside a glass bulb. A-bulbs are the old standbys; R and PAR bulbs produce a more controlled beam; silvered-bowl types diffuse light. A number of decorative bulbs are also available.

Low-voltage incandescent lighting is especially useful for accent lighting. Operating on 12 or 24 volts, these lights require transformers (which are often built into the fixtures) to step down the voltage from standard 120-volt household circuits.

Fluorescent light. Fluorescent tubes are unrivaled for energy efficiency; they also last far longer than incandescent bulbs. In some energy-conscious areas, general lighting for new kitchens *must* be fluorescent.

Older fluorescent tubes have been criticized for noise, flicker, and poor color rendition. Electronic ballasts and better fixture shielding against glare have remedied the first two problems; as for the last one, manufacturers have developed fluorescents in a wide spectrum of colors, from very warm (about 2,700 degrees K) to very cool (about 6,300 degrees K).

Quartz halogen. These bright, white newcomers are excellent for task lighting, pinpoint accenting, and other dramatic accents. Halogen is usually low-voltage but may be standard line current. The popular MR-16 bulb creates the tightest beam; for a longer reach and wider coverage, choose a PAR bulb. There's an abundance of smaller bulb shapes and sizes that fit pendants and under-cabinet strip lights.

Halogen has two disadvantages: high initial cost and its very high heat. Be sure to shop carefully: some fixtures on the market are not UL-approved.

Light fixtures really shine in this all low-voltage halogen kitchen. Wire-suspended spots and cones provide ambient light; downlights over the sink add both task lighting and decorative accents; under-cabinet strips light up countertops and backsplashes.

COMPARING LIGHT BULBS & TUBES

INCANDESCENT

A-bulb
Description. Familiar pear shape; frosted or clear.
Uses. Everyday household use.

T—Tubular
Description: Tube-shaped, from 5" long. Frosted or clear.
Uses. Appliances, cabinets, decorative fixtures.

R—Reflector
Description. White or silvered coating directs light out end of funnel-shaped bulb.
Uses. In directional fixtures; focuses light where needed.

PAR—Parabolic aluminized reflector
Description. Similar to auto headlamp; special shape and coating project light and control beam.
Uses. In recessed downlights and track fixtures.

Silvered bowl
Description. A-bulb, with silvered cap to cut glare and produce indirect light.
Uses. In track fixtures and pendants.

Low-voltage strip lights
Description. Like Christmas tree lights; in strips or tracks, or encased in flexible, waterproof plastic.
Uses. Task lighting and decoration.

FLUORESCENT

Tube
Description. Tube-shaped, 5" to 96" long. Needs special fixture and ballast.
Uses. Shadowless work light; also indirect lighting.

PL—Compact tube
Description. U-shaped with base; 5¼" to 7½" long.
Uses. In recessed downlights; some PL tubes include ballasts to replace A-bulbs.

QUARTZ HALOGEN

High-intensity
Description. Small, clear bulb with consistently high light output; used in halogen fixtures.
Uses. In specialized task lamps, torchères, and pendants.

Low-voltage MR-16 (mini-reflector)
Description. Tiny (2"-diameter) projector bulb; gives small circle of light from a distance.
Uses. In low-voltage track fixtures, mono-spots, and recessed downlights.

Low-voltage PAR
Description. Similar to auto headlight; tiny filament, shape, and coating give precise direction.
Uses. To project a small spot of light a long distance.

Professionally designed and owner-built, this renewed kitchen amply repays the effort. The design combines a raised ceiling, new skylight and bay window, a clean and functional layout, and all-new cabinetry and floor. Design: Rick Sambol.

REMODELING BASICS

Installation · Removal · Tools · Techniques

Remodeling a kitchen means different things to different people. A minor task, such as adding a row of track lights to illuminate a dark area or brightening your walls with new coverings, can transform the whole space and satisfy you with the fresh new look. Perhaps, though, you're ready to begin a major overhaul—relocate the sink, install a dishwasher and garbage disposer, move a wall, lay a tile floor, or open the ceiling with a skylight.

This chapter touches on all aspects of kitchen remodeling: you'll find information on dismantling as well as installing everything from appliances to windows. If you're planning only a few improvements, turn directly to the sections in which you're interested. Instructions for replacing wall cabinets or countertops, for example, can be found under "Cabinets & countertops" on pages 122-127. Do you need new wall coverings to complement those cabinets? Turn to the section on "Walls & ceilings," pages 117-121.

Can you do the job yourself? Our directions assume that you have some knowledge of basic tools, building terms, and techniques—how to hammer a nail, use a straightedge, and handle an adjustable wrench. If you need more detailed information on step-by-step procedures, take a look at the Sunset books *Basic Carpentry Illustrated*, *Basic Plumbing Illustrated*, and *Basic Home Wiring Illustrated*.

Before work begins

Are you ready to remodel? Before plunging into a project, you should form a clear idea of the sequence of steps necessary to complete the job, obtain any necessary permits from your local building department, and evaluate your own ability to perform each of the tasks. To do the work yourself, you'll also need to provide yourself with the proper materials and tools.

After you have a clear understanding of what's involved, you're ready to begin.

Can I do the work myself?

The level of skill required to remodel your kitchen depends on the scale of the improvements. Surface treatments—such as painting, wallpapering, replacing light fixtures, hanging cabinets, or laying resilient flooring—are within the realm of any homeowner with the rudiments of do-it-yourself ability. Some projects may require a few specialized tools, generally available from a building supply or home improvement center.

If you're still hesitant about your talents, register for some of the "how-to" classes often available through adult education programs. In such classes you'll learn basic techniques and acquire practical experience without making a costly mistake on your home.

Complex remodeling tasks—such as moving bearing walls, running new drain and vent pipes, or wiring new electrical circuits and service panels—are often best handled by professionals. Many smaller jobs within the structural, plumbing, and electrical areas, though, are within the skills of a homeowner with basic experience.

Planning your attack

As the scale of your remodeling project increases, the need for careful planning becomes more critical. Before the work begins, double-check the priorities listed below.

• Establish the sequence of jobs to be performed, and estimate the time required to complete each one.

• If you're getting professional assistance, make sure you have firm contracts and schedules with contractors, subcontractors, or other hired workers.

• Obtain all required building permits.

• Arrange for delivery of materials; be sure you have all the necessary tools on hand.

• If electricity, gas, or water must be shut off by the utility company, arrange for it before work is scheduled to begin.

• Find out where you can dispose of refuse, and secure any necessary dumping permits.

• Be sure there is a storage area available for temporarily relocating fixtures or appliances.

• Measure fixtures and appliances for clearance through doorways and up and down staircases.

Your goal is to maintain an operating kitchen during as much of the time as possible. With careful scheduling and planning, the remodeling siege can be relatively comfortable for the entire family.

How to use this chapter

The sections in this chapter are arranged in the order in which you'd proceed if you were installing an entirely new kitchen. Read consecutively, they'll give you an overview of the scope and sequence of kitchen improvements.

The first three sections survey the relatively complex subjects of structural, plumbing, and electrical systems. Whether or not you plan to do the work yourself, you'd be wise to review these sections for background information. A knowledge of your home's inner workings enables you to plan changes more effectively and to understand the reasons for seemingly arbitrary code restrictions affecting your plans.

Some of your most difficult remodeling hours may be spent tearing out old work. To minimize the effort, we've included removal procedures within the appropriate installation sections.

If you're planning only one or two simple projects, turn directly to the applicable sections for step-by-step instructions. Special features within the chapter present additional ideas and information for maximum improvement with minimum work and expense.

STEPS IN REMODELING

You can use this chart to plan the basic sequence of tasks involved in dismantling your old kitchen and installing the new one. Depending on the scale of your job and the specific materials you select, you may need to alter the suggested order. Manufacturers' instructions offer additional guidelines.

Removal sequence

1) Accessories, decorative elements
2) Furniture
3) Contents of cabinets, closets, shelves
4) Fixtures, appliances
5) Countertops, backsplashes
6) Base cabinets, wall cabinets, shelves
7) Floor materials
8) Light fixtures
9) Wall coverings

Installation sequence

1) Structural changes: walls, doors, windows, skylights
2) Rough plumbing changes
3) Electrical wiring
4) Wall and ceiling coverings
5) Light fixtures
6) Wall cabinets, base cabinets, kitchen islands, shelves
7) Countertops, backsplashes
8) Floor materials
9) Fixtures, appliances
10) Furniture
11) Decorative elements

Structural basics

Acquiring a basic understanding of your kitchen's structural shell is required homework for many kitchen improvements. Your kitchen's framework probably will conform to the pattern of the "typical kitchen," shown in the illustration below.

Starting at the base of the drawing, you'll notice the following framing members: a wooden sill resting on a foundation wall; a series of horizontal, evenly spaced floor joists; and a subfloor (usually plywood sheets) laid atop the joists. This platform supports the first-floor walls, both interior and exterior. The walls are formed by vertical, evenly spaced studs that run between a horizontal sole plate and parallel top plate. The primary wall coverings are fastened directly to the studs.

Depending upon the design of the house, one of several types of construction may be used above the kitchen walls. If there's a second story, a layer of ceiling joists rests on the walls; these joists support both the floor above and the kitchen ceiling below. A one-story house will have either an "open-beamed" ceiling—flat or pitched—or a "finished" ceiling. In simple terms, a finished ceiling covers the roof rafters and sheathing which, if exposed, would constitute an open-beamed ceiling. With a flat roof, the finished ceiling is attached directly to the rafters. The ceiling below a pitched roof is attached to joists or to a metal or wooden frame.

Removing a partition wall

Often a major kitchen remodeling means removing all or part of an interior wall to enlarge the space.

Walls that define your kitchen may be bearing or nonbearing. A bearing wall helps support the weight of the house; a nonbearing wall does not. An interior nonbearing wall, often called a partition wall, may be removed without special precautions. The procedure outlined in this section applies to partitions only. If you're considering a remodeling project that involves moving a bearing wall or any wall beneath a second story, consult an architect or contractor about problems and procedures.

How can you tell the difference in walls? All exterior walls running perpendicular to ceiling and floor joists are bearing. Normally, at least one main interior wall is also a bearing wall. If possible, climb up into the attic or crawlspace and check the ceiling joists. If they are joined over any wall, that wall is bearing. Even if joists span the entire width of the house, their midsections may be resting on a bearing wall at the point of maximum allowable span. If you have any doubts about the wall, consult an architect, contractor, or building inspector.

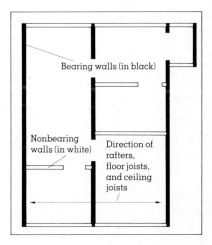

Bearing walls (in black)

Nonbearing walls (in white)

Direction of rafters, floor joists, and ceiling joists

Though removing a partition wall is not complicated, it can be quite messy. Cover the floors and furnishings, and wear a painter's mask, safety glasses, and gloves. NOTE: Check the wall for signs of electrical wiring, water and drain pipes, or heating and ventilation ducts. Any of these obstructions must be carefully rerouted before you remove the wall.

Removing wall covering. First, if there's a door in the wall, remove it from its hinges. Pry off any door trim, ceiling molding, and base molding.

The most common wall covering is gypsum wallboard nailed to wall studs. To remove it, knock holes in the wallboard with a hammer, then pull it away from the studs with a pry bar. After one surface is re-

BASIC STRUCTURAL ANATOMY

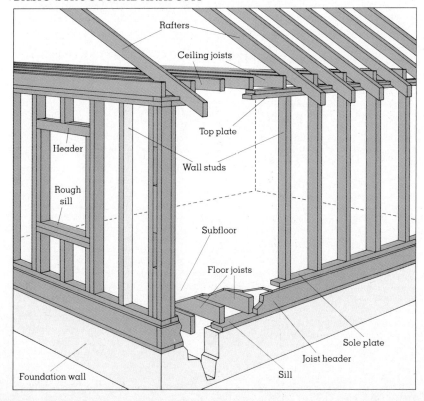

Rafters

Ceiling joists

Top plate

Header

Wall studs

Rough sill

Subfloor

Floor joists

Sole plate

Joist header

Foundation wall

Sill

... Structural basics

HOW TO REMOVE WALL FRAMING

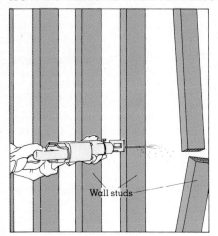

Saw through the middle of the wall studs; bend the studs sideways to free the nails from the top and sole plates.

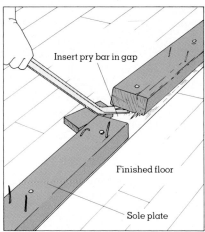

Cut gaps through the sole plate with a saw and chisel; insert a pry bar in each gap to free the sole plate.

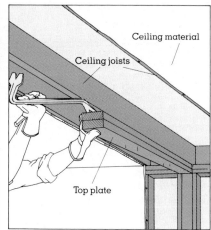

Strip ceiling materials back from the top plate, cut gaps in the plate, and pry out sections of plate.

moved, you can hit the other side from behind to knock it free.

If the wall covering is plaster and lath, chisel away the plaster until the lath backing—wood strips or metal—is exposed. You'll have to cut through the lath to break it up; then pry the lath and plaster away from the studs.

Dismantling the framing. Remove studs by sawing through the middle of each one; then, push and pull them sideways to free the nails. To get at end studs (attached to studs or nailing blocks in adjacent walls), strip wall coverings back to the bordering studs and pry loose the end stud from the side.

To remove the sole plate, saw a small section out of the middle down to the finished floor level, chisel through the remaining thickness, and insert a pry bar in the gap.

To remove a top plate that lies parallel to the joists, cut ceiling materials back to adjacent joists, and pry off the plate. If the top plate is perpendicular to the joists, cut an even 2-foot strip in the ceiling materials, making certain that you don't cut into joists; remove the plate.

Patching walls, ceilings, and floors. Wallboard and plaster aren't difficult to patch (see page 124); the real challenge lies in matching a spe-

cial texture, wallpaper, shade of paint, or well-aged floor. This is not a problem if your remodeling plans call for new wall coverings, ceiling, or flooring. In either case, see the sections on "Walls & ceilings" (pages 117–121) and "Flooring"(pages 128–133) for techniques and tips.

Framing a new wall

To separate a kitchen from an adjoining living area or to subdivide

space within the kitchen, you may need to build a new partition wall.

Framing a wall is a straightforward task, but you must measure carefully and continue to check the alignment as work progresses. The basic steps are listed below. To install a doorway, see page 100.

Plotting the location. The new wall must be anchored securely to the floor, ceiling joists, and, if possible, to wall framing on one side.

WALL FRAMING COMPONENTS

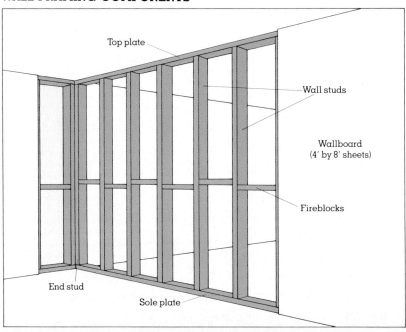

To locate the studs, try knocking with your fist along the wall until the sound changes from hollow to solid. If you have wallboard, you can use an inexpensive stud finder; often, though, the nails that hold wallboard to the studs are visible on close inspection.

To locate ceiling joists, use the same methods or, from the attic or crawlspace, drive small nails down through the ceiling on both sides of a joist to serve as reference points below. Adjacent joists and studs will be evenly spaced, usually 16 or 24 inches away from those you've located.

A wall running perpendicular to the joists will demand least effort to attach. If wall and joists will run parallel, though, try to center the wall under a single joist; otherwise, you'll need to install nailing blocks every 2 feet between two parallel joists (see illustration above right). If the side of the new wall falls between existing studs you'll need to install additional nailing blocks.

On the ceiling, mark both ends of the center line of the new wall. Measure 1¾ inches (half the width of a 2 by 4 top plate) on both sides of each mark; snap parallel lines between corresponding marks with a chalkline; the top plate will occupy the space between the lines.

Positioning the sole plate. Hang a plumb bob from each end of the lines you just marked and mark these new points on the floor. Snap two more chalklines to connect the floor points.

Cut both sole plate and top plate to the desired length. Lay the sole

HOW TO ANCHOR A TOP PLATE

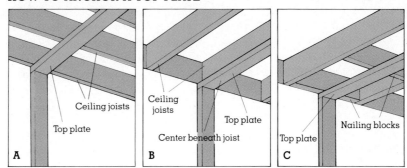

To anchor a top plate, nail to perpendicular joists (A), to the bottom of the parallel joist (B), or install nailing blocks between the parallel joists (C).

plate between the lines on the floor and nail it in place with 10-penny nails spaced every 2 feet. (If you have a masonry floor, use a masonry bit to drill holes through the sole plate every 2 or 3 feet. Then insert expansion bolts.)

If you're planning a doorway (see "Framing a doorway," page 100), don't nail through that section of the plate; it will be cut out later.

Marking stud positions. Lay the top plate against the sole plate, as shown in the illustration below. Beginning at the end that will be attached to an existing stud or to nailing blocks, measure in 1½ inches— the thickness of a 2 by 4 stud—and draw a line across both plates with a combination square. Starting once more from that end, measure and draw lines at 15¼ and 16¾ inches. From these lines, advance 16 inches at a time, drawing new lines, until the far end of both plates is reached. Each set of lines will outline the placement of a stud, with all studs

evenly spaced 16 inches "on center" (O.C.). Don't worry if the spacing at the far end is less than 16 inches. (If local codes permit, use a 24-inch spacing—you'll save lumber—and adjust the initial placement of lines to 23¼ and 24¾ inches.)

Fastening the top plate. With two helpers, lift the top plate into position between the lines (marked on the ceiling); nail it to perpendicular joists, to one parallel joist, or to nailing blocks, as shown above.

Attaching the studs. Measure and cut the studs to exact length. Attach one end stud (or both) to existing studs or to nailing blocks between studs. Lift the remaining studs into place one at a time; line them up on the marks, and check plumb with a carpenter's level. Toenail the studs to both top plate and sole plate with 8-penny nails.

Many building codes require horizontal fireblocks between studs. The number of rows depends on the code; if permitted, position blocks to provide an extra nailing surface for wall materials.

Finishing. After the studs are installed, it's time to add electrical outlets and switches (see pages 110–111), as well as new plumbing (pages 104–106). It's also time for the building inspector to check your work. Following the inspection, you can apply wall coverings of your choice (see pages 117–121), patch the ceiling, and add base moldings.

HOW TO MARK STUD POSITIONS

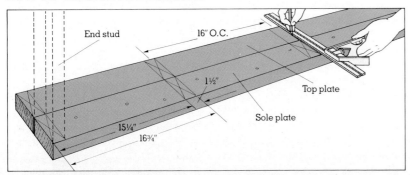

(Continued on next page)

. . . Structural basics

HOW TO FRAME A DOORWAY

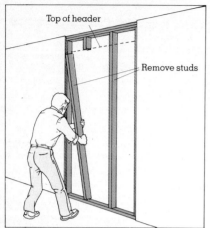

Mark and cut studs within the opening, even with the top of the new header.

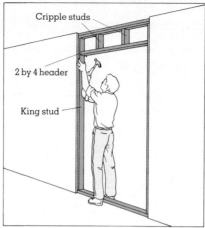

Nail the new header to the king studs; nail into ends of the new cripple studs.

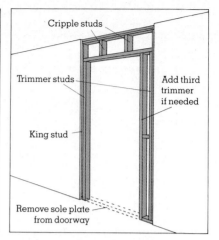

Nail trimmer studs to the king studs; block out a third trimmer, if needed.

Framing a doorway

Relocating kitchen appliances, cabinets or counters, or simply redirecting traffic flow may involve moving a door opening. Covering an existing door is relatively easy (see below). To create a new opening, it's necessary to remove wall materials, add door framing, and possibly hang a new door. Be sure the wall you plan to cut into is a nonbearing wall (see "Removing a partition wall," page 97). If the wall contains electrical wires, pipes, or ductwork, they must be rerouted.

Positioning the opening. Are you planning an open doorway, or a frame for a bifold, sliding, or standard prehung door? Determine the door type before starting work, and check the manufacturer's "rough opening" dimensions—the exact wall opening required after the new framing is in place.

You'll need to plan an opening large enough to accommodate both the rough opening and the rough door framing—an additional 1½ inches on top and sides, plus an extra ½ inch all around for shimming the typical door frame (adjusting level and plumb).

Often it's simpler to remove the wallboard from floor to ceiling between two bordering studs (the new king studs) that will remain in place. (This is the method illustrated.) In any case, you'll save work later if you can use at least one existing stud as part of the rough framing.

Regardless of the method you choose, use a carpenter's level for a straightedge, and mark the outline of the opening on the wall.

Removing wall covering and studs. First remove any base molding. Cut along the door outline with a reciprocating or keyhole saw, being careful to sever only the wallboard, not the studs beneath. Pry the wallboard away from the framing. To remove plaster and lath, chisel through the plaster to expose the lath; then cut the lath and pry it loose.

Cut the studs inside the opening to the height required for the header (see drawing above). Using a combination square, mark these studs on the face and one side, then cut carefully with a reciprocating or crosscut saw. Pry the cut studs loose from the sole plate.

Framing the opening. With wall covering and studs removed, you're ready to frame the opening. Measure and cut the header (for a partition wall you can use a 2 by 4 laid flat), and toenail it to the king studs with 8-penny nails. Nail the header to the bottoms of the cripple studs.

Cut the sole plate within the opening, and pry it away from the subfloor.

Cut trimmer studs and nail them to the king studs with 10-penny nails in a staggered pattern. You'll probably need to adjust the width by blocking out a third trimmer from one side, as shown above right. (Leave an extra ½ inch on each side for shimming if you're installing a door frame.)

Hanging the door. Bifold, swinging, or sliding pocket doors are most commonly used in kitchens. Methods of hanging doors vary considerably, depending on type. Check the manufacturer's instructions carefully before you plan the wall opening.

Even if you're not hanging a door, you'll probably want to install a preassembled door frame—consisting of a top jamb and two side jambs—to cover the rough framing.

Installing trim. When the framing is completed and the door is hung, patch the wallboard (see page 124) and install new trim (casing) around the opening. Some prehung doors have casing attached.

Closing a doorway

It's easy to eliminate an existing doorway. Simply add new studs within the opening and attach new wall coverings. The only trick is to match the present wall surface.

First, remove the casing around the opening. Then remove the door from its hinges or guide track and pry any jambs or tracks away from the rough framing.

Next, measure the gap on the floor between the existing trimmer studs; cut a length of 2 by 4 to serve as a new sole plate. Nail it to the floor with 10-penny nails. (If you have a masonry floor, attach the 2 by 4 with expansion bolts.)

Measure and cut new studs to fill the space; position one stud beneath each cripple stud. Toenail the studs to new sole plate and header with 8-penny nails. Add fireblocks between studs if required by the local code.

Strip the wall coverings back far enough to give yourself a firm nailing surface and an even edge. Then add new coverings to match the existing ones (see page 117), or resurface the entire wall. Match or replace the baseboard molding.

Window basics

Framing and hanging a window is similar to installing a door (see page 100), though in addition you must cut into the exterior siding and sheathing of the house. But the most important factor to consider is the possibility that you may be dealing with a bearing wall (see page 97). Removing studs from a bearing wall means constructing a temporary support wall before you start work and using more rigid framing than that required for partition wall openings.

An outline of basic window installation follows. For details about tools and step-by-step techniques, see the Sunset book *Windows & Skylights.*

Removing an existing window. First remove any interior and exterior trim that's not an integral part of the unit. Take out the sash, if possible (see drawing above); then remove the frame. The frame may have been nailed directly to the rough framing materials or secured by flanges or brackets.

BASIC WINDOW COMPONENTS

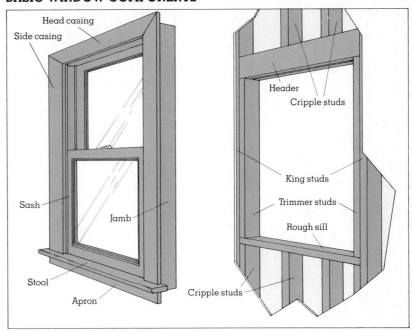

Basic window framing. Unlike rough door framing, window framing includes cripple studs at the top *and* bottom. The rough sill—a length of 2 by 4 lumber laid flat and sometimes doubled for strength—lies at the bottom edge of the opening. The top edge is bounded by the header. The header for a bearing wall opening and (depending on local codes) for any exterior wall is typically composed of matching lengths of "2-by" framing lumber turned on edge, with ½-inch-thick plywood spacers sandwiched between them. The exact size of 2-by material required depends on both the width of the window opening and your local building code.

Cutting a new opening. You'll receive a rough opening size for your new window from the manufacturer. The actual opening will be somewhat larger: add to the rough opening size the dimensions of the king studs, trimmer studs, header, and sill, plus an extra ⅜ inch on all sides for leveling and plumbing the window. Work from the inside of the house outward. If possible, complete the rough framing before opening the siding to the elements.

Installing a prehung window. A prehung window arrives with the sash already installed inside the window frame—and frequently with the exterior casing (trim) attached. To simply replace an existing window with another of the same size, first remove the interior trim and measure the rough opening; then order the new window to fit.

Using wood shims or blocks, center, level, and plumb the new window in the opening; then fasten it to the rough framing. Depending on window type, you'll either nail through a flange into the outside sheathing, screw the jambs to the header and trimmer studs, or nail through preassembled exterior trim.

Finishing touches. Your new window may need exterior casing and a drip cap. Or you may be required to install metal flashing over the unit's top edge. Thoroughly caulk the joints between the siding and the new window.

Cover the top and sides of the inside opening with casing and install a finished stool over the rough sill. Finally, add one last strip of casing (called an apron).

(Continued on page 103)

AN INTRODUCTION TO GREENHOUSE WINDOWS

Like its full-scale counterpart, a greenhouse window addition will nurture as well as showcase your favorite plants. The greenhouse window also provides a unique decorating tool: plant-laden shelves reach beyond a wall and seemingly expand an enclosed room into the open space beyond. Extending a kitchen countertop into the window unit heightens this illusion; it also can bring within reach an herb garden to inspire a cook.

Greenhouse window details

Greenhouse windows range from 3 feet square to 10 feet wide and 5 feet tall. (Units wider than 5 feet may require special framing and installation.) Standard depth is 12 to 16 inches. Preassembled units include glazing, framing, and adjustable shelving.

Choose either glass or plastic glazing; both offer a variety of finishes. Though plastic is shatter-resistant, glass is more durable and less prone to scratching. Aluminum structural sections are lightweight and maintenance-free; wood-framed units, though bulkier, offer you greater possibility in the choice of finish.

Options in greenhouse units include weatherstripping along vents to decrease cold air infiltration, screening inside vents to keep insects out, and double glazing to slow heat loss.

Other means of controlling heat loss through a greenhouse window include interior shutters and quilted window covers that isolate the unit from heated living space. For further information on insulating and shading windows, refer to the *Sunset* book *Windows & Skylights*.

Installing the window unit

Installation techniques differ, depending on local building codes, the exterior siding of your house, type of window unit, and whether or not you're replacing an existing window with a unit of the same size. Greenhouse windows can be attached to the wall around an existing opening or to an existing wooden frame.

Before purchasing a window unit, it's a good idea to study various manufacturers' specifications and installation instructions.

Adding furring strips. If your home has a wood-finished exterior such as beveled siding or shingles, you'll need to add 1 by 4 furring strips around the window frame. (For masonry, masonry veneer, or stucco, follow the manufacturers' instructions or consult a contractor.)

To attach the strips, cut the siding back to the underlying sheathing so that the furring can lie flat. If building paper covers the sheathing, leave the paper intact.

Apply a generous bed of caulking to the sheathing or building paper. Then secure the furring with nails long enough to penetrate furring, building paper, and sheathing. Nails should extend into the studs or header a distance equal to twice the thickness of the furring. Set the nail heads below the furring surface.

Mounting the greenhouse window. With helpers holding the unit in place, level the window. Temporarily nail the unit in place and check the level again. Attach the window unit with screws long enough to penetrate the mounting flange, furring, sheathing, building paper, and at least an inch into the studs and header.

Finishing details. For units wider than 5 feet, bracing between the base and wall is recommended. Caulk the seams between the flange and furring and between the furring and siding. If you like, you can cover the base of the window with tile or finish it to match an adjacent countertop.

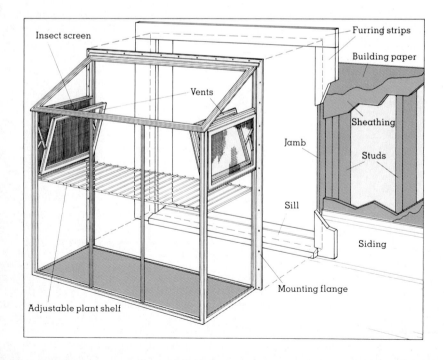

Insect screen
Vents
Jamb
Sill
Mounting flange
Adjustable plant shelf
Furring strips
Building paper
Sheathing
Studs
Siding

... Structural basics

Skylight basics

Installing a skylight in a pitched roof with asphalt or wood shingles is a two-part process: you cut and frame openings in both roof and ceiling, and connect the two openings with a vertical or angled light shaft. (You don't even need a light shaft for a flat roof or open-beamed ceiling, which requires only a single opening.) A brief description of the skylight installation sequence follows; for a complete discussion of required techniques and tools, see the *Sunset book Windows & Skylights.*

Marking the openings. Using the rough opening measurements supplied by the manufacturer, mark the location of the ceiling opening; then drive nails up through the four corners and center so they'll be visible in the attic or crawlspace. From the attic, check for obstructions, shifting the location if necessary. You'll save work if you can use one or two ceiling joists as the edges of your opening.

With a plumb bob, transfer the ceiling marks to the underside of the roof; again, drive nails up through the roofing materials to mark the location. If you run into obstructions on the roof, change the position slightly and use an angled light shaft to connect the two openings.

Framing the roof opening. On a day with zero probability of rain, cut and frame the roof opening. Exercise extreme caution when working on the roof; if the pitch is steep or if you have a tile or slate roof, you might consider leaving this part to professionals.

When you work with a skylight designed to be mounted on a curb frame, build the curb first; 2 by 6 lumber is commonly used. (If your skylight has an integral curb or is self-flashing, you can skip this step.)

To determine the actual size of the opening you need to cut, add the dimensions of any framing materials (see below) to the rough opening size marked by the nails. You may need to remove some extra shingles

BASIC SKYLIGHT COMPONENTS

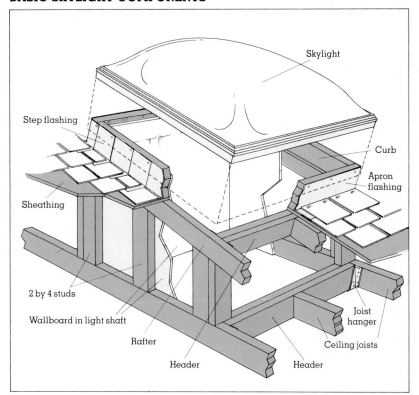

or roofing materials down to the sheathing to accommodate the flashing of a curb-mounted unit or the flange of a self-flashing unit.

Cut the roof opening in successive layers: roofing materials first, sheathing next, and finally any necessary rafters. Before cutting the rafters, support them by 2 by 4s nailed to the ceiling joists below.

To frame the opening, you'll need double headers and possibly trimmers. Install the headers with double joist hangers.

If you're installing a curb-mounted unit, position and flash the curb. Toenail the curb to the rafters or trimmers and to the headers. Pay special attention to the manufacturer's instructions concerning directions for flashing.

Mounting the skylight. For a curb-mounted unit, secure the skylight to the top of the curb with nails and a sealant. Set a self-flashing unit in roofing cement, then nail through the flange directly to the roof sheathing. Coat the joints and nail holes with more roofing cement.

Opening the ceiling. Double-check your original ceiling marks against the roof opening and the intended angle of the light shaft. Cut through the ceiling materials and then sever the joists. Support joists to be cut—do this by bracing them against adjacent joists. Frame the opening in the same manner used for the roof opening.

Building a light shaft. Measure the distance between the ceiling headers and roof headers at each corner and at 16-inch intervals between the corners. Cut studs to fit the measurements and install them as illustrated above. This provides a nailing surface for wall coverings.

Final touches. Insulate the spaces between studs in the light shaft before fastening wall coverings to the studs. Painting wallboard white maximizes reflected light.

Trim the ceiling opening with molding strips. Adding a plastic ceiling panel (either manufactured or cut to size) helps diffuse light evenly.

Plumbing basics

Do you know how your plumbing system works? If not, the kitchen is a good place to start learning, for the plumbing here is much less complicated than in other areas—bathrooms, for instance.

A plumbing overview

Three complementary sets of pipes work together to fill your home's plumbing needs: the drain-waste and vent (DWV) systems, and the water supply system. In the typical kitchen, these pipes serve the "sink complex"—the sink and related appliances, such as the dishwasher and garbage disposer.

The supply system. Water that eventually arrives at your kitchen faucet enters the house from the public water main or from a source on the property. At the water service entrance, the main supply line divides in two—one line branching off to be heated by the water heater,

the other remaining as cold water. The two pipes usually run parallel below the first-floor level until they reach the vicinity of a group of fixtures, then head up through the wall or floor. Sometimes the water supply—hot, cold, or both—passes through a water softener or filter (see drawing below) before reaching the fixtures.

Drain-waste and vent systems. The drain-waste pipes channel waste water and solid wastes to the sewer line. Vent pipes carry away sewer gas and maintain atmospheric pressure in drainpipes and fixture traps.

Every house has a main soil stack that serves a dual function: below the level of the fixtures, it is your home's primary drainpipe; at its upper end, which protrudes through the roof, the stack becomes a vent. Drainpipes from individual fixtures, as well as larger branch drains, connect to the main stack. A

fixture or fixture group located on a branch drain far from the main stack will have a secondary vent stack of its own rising to the roof.

The sink complex. Generally, a single set of vertical supply pipes and one drainpipe serve the entire kitchen. For both convenience and economy, fixtures and appliances that require water usually are adjacent to the sink. Supply pipes for a dishwasher, hot water dispenser, and automatic ice maker branch off the main hot and cold supply lines leading to the sink faucet. Similarly, the dishwasher and disposer share the sink's trap and drainpipe. The hot water dispenser discharges directly into the sink.

Roughing-in new plumbing

You will need to add new plumbing to your kitchen if you move your present sink and related appliances, plumb a sink into a new

A PLUMBING OVERVIEW

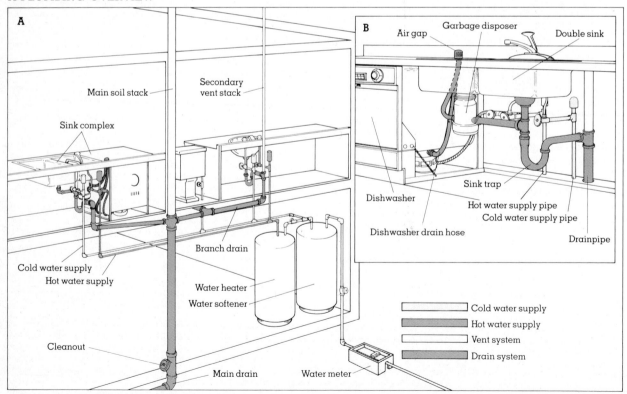

Your kitchen's plumbing is part of a coordinated system of hot and cold supply pipes leading water to fixtures and appliances, and drain-waste and vent pipes carrying wastes and gases away (A). Kitchen plumbing is commonly concentrated in the "sink complex" area (B).

kitchen island, or add a new fixture—such as a second sink.

For basic pipefitting techniques, refer to the *Sunset* book *Basic Plumbing Illustrated*. With a little experience, you may be able to handle these jobs yourself. If you have doubts about your abilities, consider hiring a professional to rough-in the new pipes. By referring to pages 134–141, you can hook up the fixtures or appliances.

Mapping your present system. If you're considering a plumbing change, you'll first need a detailed map of the present plumbing. Begin your investigation from an unfinished basement or crawlspace or, if necessary, from the attic or roof. Locate the main stack, branch drains, and any secondary stacks. Positioning yourself directly below or above the kitchen, try to determine whether the sink complex is tied directly into the main stack or connected to a branch drain with its own vent. Find the spot where vertical supply lines branch off from horizontal lines and head up into a wall or the floor.

Extending DWV pipes. Your plans to relocate a sink or add a new fixture depend on the feasibility of extending present DWV pipes. Plumbing codes, both national and local, are quite specific about the following: the size of the drainpipe or

branch drain serving the kitchen sink complex or any new fixture requiring drainage; the distance (called the "critical distance") from the traps to the main stack, secondary stack, or other vent; and the point where a new drainpipe or branch drain ties into the branch drain or main stack.

A proposed fixture located within a few feet of the main stack (check local codes for the exact distance) usually can be drained and vented directly by the stack. New fixtures distant from the stack probably will require a new branch drain beneath the floor, running either to the stack or to an existing cleanout in the main drain (see drawing below); you'll also need to run a new secondary stack up to the roof.

The drainpipe required for a kitchen sink complex normally has a diameter of at least 1½ inches (2 inches if you also plan to vent directly into the stack). Minimum vent size for a secondary stack is commonly 1¼ inches, unless a dishwasher installed without a separate air gap necessitates a larger pipe.

Your present DWV pipes probably are made of cast iron, with "hub" or "bell-and-spigot" ends joined by molten lead and oakum. To extend the system, you may substitute "hubless" fittings (consisting of neoprene gaskets and stainless steel clamps), which are simpler to install.

Since plastic is considerably lighter than cast iron and is easily joined with solvent cement, you may want to use ABS (acrylonitrile-butadiene-styrene) or PVC (polyvinyl chloride) pipe in your extension. First check the local code; many areas prohibit the use of plastic pipe.

Extending supply pipes. Because no venting is required, extending sup-

PIPES & FITTINGS

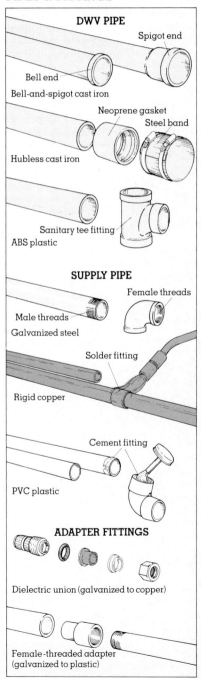

HOW TO EXTEND YOUR PLUMBING SYSTEM

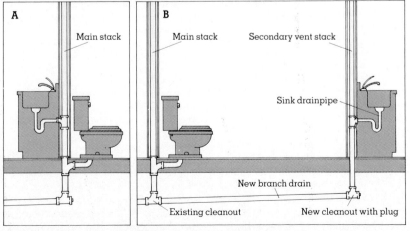

To drain kitchen plumbing additions, you can either (A) tap into the present main stack, if nearby, or (B) install a new branch drain and secondary vent stack.

... Plumbing basics

ply pipes is a much easier task than extending the DWV system. The selection of correctly sized pipes, as outlined in detail by local codes, depends equally on the type of fixture to be added, the volume of water it demands, and the length of the new pipe.

Your home's supply pipes most likely are either galvanized steel (referred to as "galvanized" or "iron" pipe) connected by threaded fittings, or rigid copper joined with soldered fittings. Some local codes permit the use of plastic supply lines; special adapters will enable you to convert from one material to another (see page 105).

Routing new pipes. Ideally, new drainpipes should be routed below the kitchen floor. They can be suspended from floor joists by pipe hangers, inserted in the space between parallel joists, or threaded through notches or holes drilled in perpendicular joists. If you have a finished basement, you'll need to cut into the ceiling to thread pipes between or through joists, hide the pipes with a dropped ceiling, or box them in.

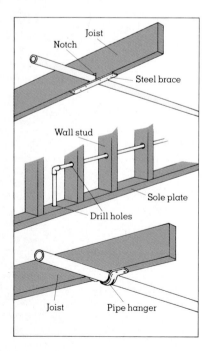

Drainpipes must slope away from fixtures; a minimum slope of ¼ inch per foot is usually required.

A new vent stack must be installed inside an existing wall (a big job), built into a new or "thickened" wall (see "Building a wet wall," below), or concealed in a closet or cabinet. In mild climates, an enclosed vent may also run up the exterior of the house, within a box.

Supply pipes normally follow drainpipes, but for convenience, can be routed directly up through the wall or floor from main horizontal lines below. Supply pipes should run parallel to each other, at least 6 inches apart.

Building a wet wall. The main soil stack, and often a secondary stack, are commonly hidden inside an oversize house wall called a "wet wall."

Unlike an ordinary 2 by 4 stud wall (shown on page 98), a wet wall has a sole plate and top plate built from 2 by 6 or 2 by 8 lumber. Additionally, the 2 by 4 studs are set in pairs, on edge, as shown below. This construction creates maximum space inside the wall for large DWV pipes (which often are wider than a standard wall) and for the fittings which are wider yet.

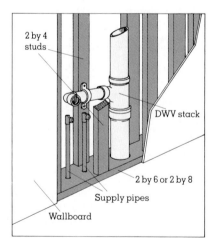

You can also "fur out" an existing wall to hide added pipes—attach new 2 by 4s to the old ones, then add new wall coverings (see above right). Similarly, a new branch drain that can't run below the floor may be hidden by furring strips laid beside the pipe and covered with

new flooring materials. (For flooring details, see page 128–133.)

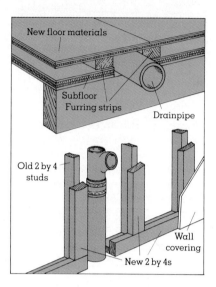

Gas system basics

When you convert from electricity to gas or simply relocate a gas appliance, keep in mind a few basic guidelines.

Materials approved for gas supply vary with the area and the type of gas. The most universally accepted materials are threaded pipe of galvanized steel, and "black pipe" (steel pipe without galvanizing). Heavier grades of copper pipe used for plumbing systems (types K and L) are also permitted in some areas.

The plumbing code, or separate gas code, will specify pipe size according to cubic foot capacity and the length of pipe between the meter or storage tank and the appliance. All gas appliances should have a numerical rating in BTUs per hour stamped on the nameplate. To convert BTUs to cubic feet, figure 1,000 BTUs to 1 cubic foot; for example, 65,000 BTUs = 65 cubic feet.

Each appliance must have a nearby code-approved shutoff valve with a straight handle, to turn off gas in an emergency.

There's no room for error when installing a gas system. It's advisable to have a professional make the installation. You must, in any case, have the work inspected and tested before the gas is turned on.

Electrical basics

What may appear to be a hopelessly tangled maze of wires running through the walls and ceiling of your home is actually a well-organized system of circuits. In your kitchen, those circuits serve the light fixtures, switches, and power outlets. Some circuits run directly to large appliances.

This section explains the electrical system in relation to kitchen lighting and appliances, and offers techniques for basic electrical improvements. More detailed step-by-step instructions may be found in the *Sunset* book *Basic Home Wiring Illustrated*. For details on installing light fixtures, see pages 112–116.

Should you do your own electrical work? It's not always permitted. Local building departments restrict the extent and type of new wiring a homeowner may undertake. In some areas, for example, you may not be permitted to add a new circuit to the service panel. Or if the wiring inside the walls of an older home is the knob-and-tube variety, local regulations may require that new hookups be made by licensed electricians. When restrictions don't apply, problems can still crop up. If you have any doubt about how to proceed, it's best to hire a professional.

Before you do any of the work yourself, talk with your building department's electrical inspector about local codes, the National Electrical Code (NEC), and your area's requirements concerning permits and inspections.

Understanding your system

Today most homes have what's called "three-wire" service. The utility company connects three wires to your service entrance panel. Each of two "hot" wires supplies electricity at approximately 120 volts. During normal operation, the third—or "neutral"—wire is maintained at zero volts. (Don't be misled, though, by the harmless sound of "neutral"; all three wires are "live.")

Three-wire service provides both 120-volt and 240-volt capabilities. One hot wire and the neutral

wire combine to supply 120 volts, used for most household applications such as lights and small appliances. Both hot wires and the neutral wire can complete a 120/240-volt circuit for such needs as an electric range or clothes dryer.

Many older homes have only two-wire service, with one hot wire at 120 volts and one neutral wire. Two-wire service does not have 240-volt capability.

Service entrance panel. This panel is the control center for your electrical system. Inside you'll find the main disconnect (main fuses or main circuit breaker), the fuses or circuit breakers protecting individual circuits, and the grounding connection for the entire system.

After entering the panel and passing through the main disconnect, each hot wire connects to one of two "bus bars," as shown below. These bars accept the amount of current permitted by the main disconnect and allow you to divide that current into smaller branch circuits. The neutral wire is attached to a neutral bus bar, which is in direct contact with the earth through the grounding electrode conductor.

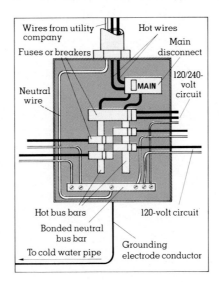

Your home may also have one or more subpanels from which branch circuits originate. A subpanel is an extension of the service entrance panel; the two are connected by hot and neutral "subfeeds."

Simple circuitry. The word "circuit" represents the course that electric current travels; carried by the hot wire, it passes from the service entrance panel or subpanel to one or more devices using electricity (such as a group of light fixtures), then returns to the panel by way of the neutral wire. The devices are normally connected by parallel wiring, as shown below. The hot and neutral wires run continuously from one fixture or outlet box to another; separate wires branch off to individual devices.

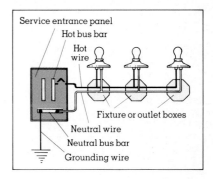

Each 120-volt branch circuit consists of one hot wire and one neutral wire. The hot wire originates at a branch circuit fuse or circuit breaker connected to one of the hot bus bars. A 120/240-volt circuit, which requires both hot wires, is connected through the fuse or breaker to both hot bus bars. All neutral conductors originate at the neutral bus bar inside the panel.

Grounding prevents shock. The NEC requires that every circuit have a grounding system. Grounding ensures that all metal parts of a wiring system will be maintained at zero volts. In the event of a short circuit, a grounding wire carries current back to the service entrance panel and ensures that the fuse or circuit breaker will open, shutting off the flow of current.

The grounding wire for each circuit is attached to the neutral bus bar and then is run with the hot and neutral wires; individual "jumper" wires branch off to ground individual metal devices and boxes as required.

(Continued on next page)

... Electrical basics

Planning electrical improvements

Before you start daydreaming about new track lighting, a dishwasher, or a disposer, you'll need to know whether your present system can handle an additional load.

Service type and rating. First, determine your present type of electrical service. Looking through the window of your meter, you'll see several numbers on the faceplate: 120V indicates two-wire service; 240V indicates three-wire service that provides both 120-volt and 240-volt capabilities.

Your electrical system is also rated for the maximum amount of current (measured in amperes—or "amps") it can carry. This "service rating," determined by the size of the service entrance equipment, should be stamped on the main fuses or circuit breaker. If your system doesn't have a main disconnect, call your utility company or building department for the rating.

Codes. Requirements for electrical circuits serving a modern kitchen and dining area are clearly prescribed by the NEC. Plug-in outlets and switches for small appliances

and the refrigerator must be served by a minimum of two 20-amp circuits. Light fixtures are not connected to these circuits, but they share one or more 15-amp circuits. These latter circuits also run, as a rule, to the dining room, living room, or other adjacent space.

If you're installing a dishwasher and/or disposer, you'll need a separate 20-amp circuit for each. Most electric ranges use an individual 50-amp, 120/240-volt major appliance circuit. Wall ovens and a separate cooktop may share a 50-amp circuit.

Tapping into a present circuit. A circuit can be tapped wherever there's an accessible housing box (see "Selecting a power source," page 109). Because of code restrictions, though, you must tap the correct *type* of circuit.

You also must determine that the circuit you hope to tap doesn't already carry the maximum load allowed. For help in mapping your circuits, consult an electrician, your building department, or the *Sunset* book *Basic Home Wiring Illustrated*.

Adding a new circuit. When an existing circuit can't handle a new load

or when a new appliance requires its own circuit, you can often add a new circuit or a subpanel. However, your present house load combined with the proposed addition still must not exceed your service rating.

To help calculate the house load, the NEC has established representative values and formulas based on typical electrical usage. For further aid check with your building department's electrical inspector.

Older homes with two-wire service of less than 100 amps simply can't support many major improvements. To add a new oven or dishwasher you may need to increase your service type and rating, which means replacing the service entrance equipment.

Working with wire

To wire basic extensions to your present electrical circuits, you'll need a few tools and materials, a knack for making wire splices, and the patience to route new wire from box to box and then patch wall and ceiling materials. For work on this scale, an electrical permit will probably be required.

Here's the most important rule for all do-it-yourself electricians:

TYPICAL KITCHEN CIRCUITS

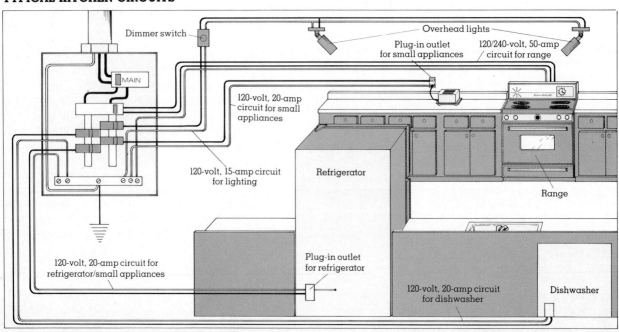

Dimmer switch

Overhead lights

Plug-in outlet for small appliances

120/240-volt, 50-amp circuit for range

MAIN

120-volt, 20-amp circuit for small appliances

120-volt, 15-amp circuit for lighting

Refrigerator

Range

120-volt, 20-amp circuit for refrigerator/small appliances

Plug-in outlet for refrigerator

120-volt, 20-amp circuit for dishwasher

Dishwasher

Never work on any "live" circuit, fixture, plug-in outlet, or switch. Your life may depend on it.

Before starting to work, you must disconnect the circuit at its source, either in the service entrance panel or in a separate subpanel. If fuses protect your circuits, remove the appropriate fuse. In a panel or subpanel equipped with circuit breakers, switch the breaker to the *OFF* position to disconnect the circuit, then tape over the switch for extra safety.

Selecting a power source. A circuit can be extended from a present outlet box, fixture box, switch box, or junction box. The one exception is a switch box without a neutral wire *(see pages 110–111).*

Before deciding which box to tap, consider how you'll route wire to the new switch, outlet, or fixture. Look for the easiest paths behind walls, above ceilings, and under floors. Then choose the most convenient power source.

The box tapped must be large enough to accommodate the new wires (minimum box sizes are specified by the NEC) and must have a knockout hole through which you can thread the cable. If your box doesn't meet these requirements, replace it with one that does.

Preparing for new boxes. Housing boxes—capped with fixture canopies, outlet plates, or switch plates—come in many shapes and sizes. For outlets, switches, and fixtures weighing 5 pounds or less, choose "cut-in" boxes, which need not be secured to studs or joists. (If wall or ceiling coverings haven't been in-

stalled, you can nail a "flange" box to studs or joists.) Unless codes prohibit the use of plastic, you may select either plastic or metal boxes. Metal boxes, though sturdier, must be grounded; plastic boxes cost less and need not be grounded.

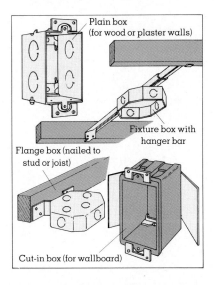

Plain box (for wood or plaster walls)

Fixture box with hanger bar

Flange box (nailed to stud or joist)

Cut-in box (for wallboard)

Position the box between studs or joists in an area free of pipes and other wires. To find a suitable location, first cut off power to all circuits that might run behind the wall or ceiling where you're placing the box. Drill a small test hole, and probe behind the surface with a length of stiff wire until you find a space.

Trace the outline of the box on the wall or ceiling, omitting any protruding brackets. Drill a starter hole in one corner, then make the cutout with a keyhole or saber saw.

Routing new cable. Your new "wires" actually will be self-contained lengths of nonmetallic sheathed ca-

ble. A single cable contains either one or two hot wires, a neutral wire, and a grounding wire, each wrapped in its own insulation. To insure the best splices, use only cable containing all-copper wire. Check local codes for the correct cable size.

After cutting the holes but before mounting the boxes, you must run cable from the power source to each new box location. Access from an unfinished basement, an unfloored attic, or a garage adjacent to the kitchen makes it easy to run cable either on top of joists and studs or through holes drilled in them.

If walls and ceilings are covered on both sides, you'll have to "fish" the cable (see drawing below). Use a fish tape (buy it at a plumbing supply or hardware store—or you may find one to rent) or a length of stiff wire.

Attaching new boxes. After you've routed the new cable, secure each housing box to the ceiling or wall. Slip a cable connector onto the end of the cable and insert it through a knockout in the box. Fasten the connector to the box, leaving 6 to 8 inches of cable free for making the connections. Then mount the box.

(Continued on next page)

HOW TO ROUTE CABLE TO FIXTURES

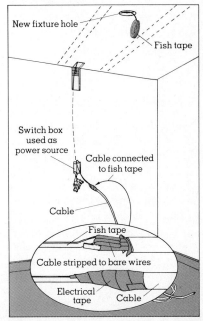

New fixture hole

Fish tape

Switch box used as power source

Cable connected to fish tape

Cable

Fish tape

Cable stripped to bare wires

Electrical tape

Cable

HOW TO ROUTE CABLE TO OUTLETS

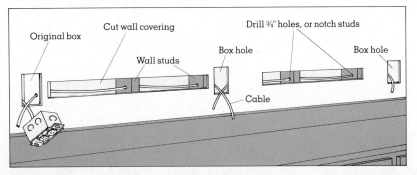

Original box

Cut wall covering

Wall studs

Drill ¾" holes, or notch studs

Box hole

Box hole

Cable

... **Electrical basics**

HOW TO WIRE INTO THE POWER SOURCE

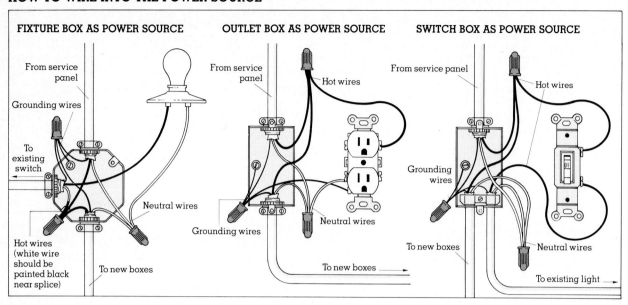

FIXTURE BOX AS POWER SOURCE

From service panel

Grounding wires

To existing switch

Neutral wires

Hot wires (white wire should be painted black near splice)

To new boxes

OUTLET BOX AS POWER SOURCE

From service panel

Hot wires

Grounding wires

Neutral wires

To new boxes

SWITCH BOX AS POWER SOURCE

From service panel

Hot wires

Grounding wires

Neutral wires

To new boxes

To existing light

Wiring into the power source. Connections to three types of boxes used as power sources are illustrated above. A fourth option is a junction box, where wires are simply joined.

Wirenuts join and protect the stripped ends of spliced wires within housing boxes. The correct wirenut size depends on the number and size of wires you'll be joining.

NOTE: For simplicity's sake, the wires illustrated on these pages are color-coded as follows:

• Hot wires: thick black or gold.

• Neutral wires: thick white.

• Grounding wires: narrow black.

Actual hot wires are usually black or red, but may be any color other than white, gray, or green. Actual neutral wires are white or gray; grounding wires are bare copper or aluminum, green, or, in rare cases, black.

Occasionally a white wire will be used as a hot wire, in which case it should be taped or painted black near terminals and splices for easy identification.

To join wires with a wirenut, follow this sequence: (A) strip 1 inch of insulation from the wire ends, and twist the ends clockwise 1½ turns; (B) snip ⅜ to ½ inch off the twisted wires; then (C) screw the wirenut clockwise onto the wires.

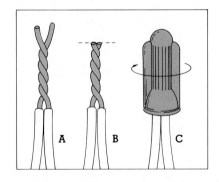

Wiring plug-in outlets

Plug-in outlets can be wired in several ways. You may want to keep one or both halves electrically live at all times so that appliances can be controlled by their own switches. Or you may wish to turn one or both halves on and off with wall switches—for example, to control a garbage disposer.

Outlets should be evenly distributed between small appliance circuits in the kitchen area. For example, if there are two small appli-

ance circuits and eight outlets in the area, each circuit should serve four outlets.

All outlets for 15 or 20-amp circuits must be of the grounding type shown at the top of page 111. Outlets are rated for a specific amperage and voltage; be sure to buy the type you need.

If you want to add a grounded outlet to a circuit that does not contain a grounding wire, you'll have to run a separate wire from the new outlet to a nearby cold water pipe (see page 112). Check the neutral bus bar at the service entrance panel to find out whether the circuit has a grounding wire.

The drawings at the top of page 111 show two common ways to wire new outlets. The housing boxes are assumed to be metal; if you choose plastic, there's no need to ground the boxes, but you'll have to attach a grounding wire to each outlet. Simply loop the end of the wire under the grounding screw.

Wiring new switches

Both "single-pole" and "three-way" switches are used in homes. A single-pole switch may control one or more light fixtures or outlets; two three-way switches in different lo-

HOW TO WIRE PLUG-IN OUTLETS

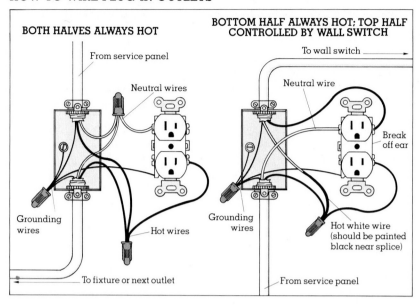

BOTH HALVES ALWAYS HOT

From service panel

Neutral wires

Grounding wires

Hot wires

To fixture or next outlet

BOTTOM HALF ALWAYS HOT; TOP HALF CONTROLLED BY WALL SWITCH

To wall switch

Neutral wire

Break off ear

Grounding wires

Hot white wire (should be painted black near splice)

From service panel

cations may also control one or more fixtures or outlets.

Like outlets, each switch must have the same amp and voltage rating as the circuit. Remember when wiring that *switches are installed only along hot wires.*

The switches shown on this page have no grounding wires. Because the plastic toggles used on most home switches are shockproof, these switches don't need to be grounded. If switches are housed inside metal boxes, the boxes do need to be grounded. When installing a plastic switch box at the end of a circuit, secure the end of the grounding wire between the switch bracket and the mounting screw.

Single-pole switches. These switches have two screw terminals of the same color (usually brass) for wire connections, and a definite vertical orientation. You should be able to read the words ON and OFF embossed on the toggle. It makes no difference which hot wire goes to which terminal. Because of code limitations on the number of wires that a switch box may contain, the cable sometimes must run to the fixture first and at other times to the switch. Check your local codes.

Three-way switches. These switches have two screw terminals of the same color (brass or silver) and one of a darker color, identified by the word "common." Either end of a three-way switch can go up. It's important to observe, though, which terminal is the odd-colored one; it may be located differently than in the drawing below.

To wire a pair of three-way switches, first connect the hot wire from the service entrance panel or subpanel to the odd-colored terminal of one switch; then connect the hot wire from the fixture or outlet to the odd-colored terminal of the other switch. Wire the remaining terminals by running hot wires from the two same-colored terminals on one switch to the two same-colored terminals on the other.

HOW TO WIRE THREE-WAY SWITCHES

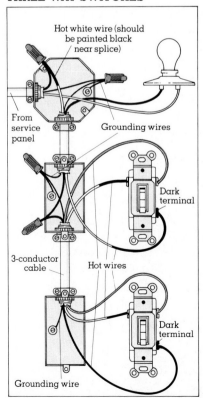

Hot white wire (should be painted black near splice)

From service panel

Grounding wires

Dark terminal

3-conductor cable

Hot wires

Dark terminal

Grounding wire

HOW TO WIRE SINGLE-POLE SWITCHES

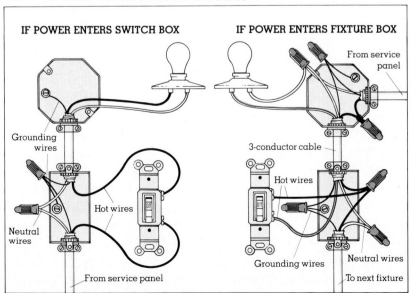

IF POWER ENTERS SWITCH BOX

Grounding wires

Hot wires

Neutral wires

From service panel

IF POWER ENTERS FIXTURE BOX

From service panel

3-conductor cable

Hot wires

Grounding wires

Neutral wires

To next fixture

Light fixtures

Kitchen lighting needs fall into two categories—general and task lighting. Both incandescent and fluorescent lights can be used to satisfy either need. You'll probably implement lighting with one or more of the three popular types of fixtures: surface-mounted, track, and recessed downlight or panel.

Replacing an existing light fixture with one of the same type usually is a minor operation; you simply unscrew the fixture from its housing box, disconnect the wires of the old fixture, and hook up new wires. Adding a new fixture where there was none is a more complex process. After running new cable from a power source, you must install a housing box and a switch to control the fixture. Do you feel that's out of your league? For help, see "Electrical basics" on pages 107–111.

Normally, you won't need an electrical permit to simply exchange fixtures or switches. You may need a permit and professional help for a new installation.

Installing surface-mounted fixtures

Surface-mounted fixtures are either attached directly to a fixture box in the wall or ceiling or suspended from the box by chains or cord. New fixtures usually come with their own mounting hardware, adaptable to any existing fixture box. Sometimes, though, the weight of the new fixture or the wiring necessary for proper grounding requires that you replace the box before installing the fixture.

Attaching fixtures. The weight of the fixture determines how it will be attached. Boxes for fixtures weighing more than 5 pounds must be nailed to a joist or hung on a bar between joists. If the fixture weighs more than 30 pounds, the fixture should be connected to the box's metallic stud with a hickey or reducing nut.

Grounding metal fixtures. The National Electrical Code requires that all incandescent and fluorescent fixtures with exposed metal parts be grounded.

If the fixture box itself is grounded (see below), the nipple or screws holding the fixture to the box will ground the fixture. There's one exception: a cord or chain-hung fixture needs a grounding wire run from the socket to the box, as shown below. Most new fixtures are prewired with a grounding wire.

If the fixture box is not grounded (as is the case when your present house wiring includes no grounding wire), you'll have to extend a grounding wire from the box to the nearest cold water pipe. To do this, you'll need a length of bare #12 copper wire, a grounding strap, and enough patience to route the wire so that it won't be an eyesore. Wrap one end of the wire around the grounding screw or around the nipple or screw holding the fixture to the box, and secure the other end to the screw that holds the strap to the pipe.

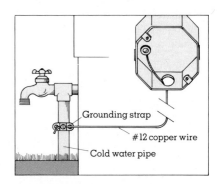

Grounding strap
#12 copper wire
Cold water pipe

Replacing fixtures. Whether you're replacing an old fixture with the same type or with a new fluorescent unit, the steps are the same.

First, disconnect the circuit by removing the fuse or switching the circuit breaker to OFF. Carefully remove the glass shade, if any, from the old fixture. Unscrew the canopy

SURFACE-MOUNTED FIXTURES

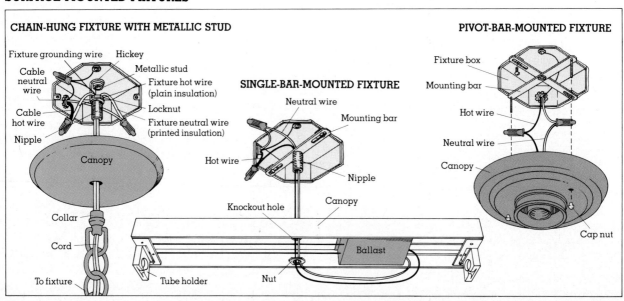

CHAIN-HUNG FIXTURE WITH METALLIC STUD

Fixture grounding wire
Hickey
Cable neutral wire
Metallic stud
Fixture hot wire (plain insulation)
Cable hot wire
Locknut
Fixture neutral wire (printed insulation)
Nipple
Canopy
Collar
Cord
To fixture

SINGLE-BAR-MOUNTED FIXTURE
Neutral wire
Mounting bar
Hot wire
Nipple
Knockout hole
Canopy
Ballast
Tube holder
Nut

PIVOT-BAR-MOUNTED FIXTURE
Fixture box
Mounting bar
Hot wire
Neutral wire
Canopy
Cap nut

TRACK SYSTEMS

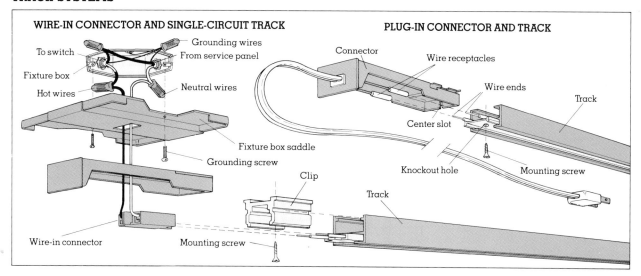

WIRE-IN CONNECTOR AND SINGLE-CIRCUIT TRACK

PLUG-IN CONNECTOR AND TRACK

from the fixture box; detach the mounting bar if there is one. Have a helper hold the fixture to keep it from falling.

Now, make a sketch of how the wires are connected. If they're spliced with wirenuts, unscrew them and untwist the wires. If the wires are spliced only with electrician's tape, simply unwind the tape. New splices will be covered with wirenuts. Lay the old fixture aside.

As your helper holds up the new fixture, match its wires to the old wires as shown in your sketch. Splice with wirenuts *(see page 110).*

Secure the new fixture by reversing the steps you took to loosen the original, using any new hardware included with the fixture. If you need to patch the wall or ceiling, see page 124.

Adding new fixtures. Installing a new surface-mounted fixture is much like replacing one, once the cable has been routed from a power source and the fixture box and switch installed.

New nonmetallic cable routed to the box should include a grounding wire, which is attached to the box's grounding screw. If more than one cable enters the box (for example, a separate cable may be connected to the switch box), you'll need to attach the end of a short length of #12 wire (a "jumper") to the ground-

ing screw and splice its other end to the ends of the grounding wires in the cables. Cap the splice with a wirenut.

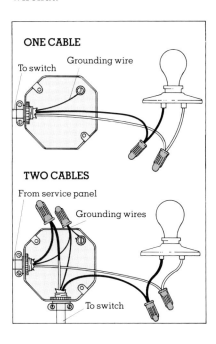

ONE CABLE

TWO CABLES

A cord or chain-hung fixture must also have a grounding wire run from the socket to the box *(see page 112).*

Match the box's wires to those of the new fixture—black wire to black, white to white, as shown at left. Cap all splices with wirenuts. Then mount the fixture with the hardware specified by the manufacturer.

Installing track systems

Track systems are mounted, either directly or with mounting clips, to the wall or ceiling. Power is provided from a fixture box or through a cord plugged into an existing outlet. Tracks are often wired into two separate circuits controlled by two switches. For greater flexibility of light level and placement, install one switch plus a dimmer switch *(see page 115).*

Connecting the system. A plug-in connector, which includes a 12-foot cord and a lamp plug, lets you place a track wherever the cord will reach an outlet. Plug-in connectors are available only with single-circuit tracks.

A track system with a wire-in connector is hooked up directly to a fixture box. You may be able to use an existing box, or you may have to install a new one *(see pages 108–109).* In either case, you'll need as many wall switches as your track has circuits. If you're simply replacing a fixture with a single-circuit track system, you can use the wall switch already wired to the old fixture, or replace that switch with a dimmer.

Mounting the track. Once the power is tapped and the proper switches are installed, it's time to attach the track connector to the ceiling, wall, or fixture box *(see drawing above).*

(Continued on next page)

... Light fixtures

For attaching a track or mounting clips to the ceiling or wall, you'll use screws or toggle bolts in predrilled holes. To lay out and drill the necessary holes, line up a chalkline or the edge of a yardstick with the center slot of the connector; snap or draw a line to the proposed end of the track.

Setting a length of track beside the line, mark along the line the positions of the knockout holes in the roof of the track. These marks show you where to drill.

Because a plug-in connector lies flush against the wall or ceiling surface, you can attach the track directly to the surface. Slip the two bare wire ends of the first length of track into the connector receptacles; secure the track with screws or toggle bolts. Proceed in a similar manner with the remaining lengths of track.

A wire-in connector holds the ends of the track ¼ to ½ inch away from the mounting surface. You'll need special clips to hold the track at the same level. Once clips are screwed or bolted to the ceiling or wall, slip the first length of track into the connector; press it, and succeeding lengths, into the clips.

Installing recessed fixtures

Common recessed fixtures include incandescent circular or square downlights and larger fluorescent ceiling or "troffer" panels. You'll need to cut a hole in the ceiling between the joists, or remove tiles or panels from a suspended ceiling, to install either type. Larger fixtures may also require 2 by 4 blocking between joists for support.

Recessed fixtures need several inches of clearance above the finished ceiling. They're most easily installed below an unfinished attic or crawlspace. Because of the heat generated by many downlights, you must allow adequate air flow around the fixture; remove insulation within 3 inches of the fixture and make sure that no combustible materials are within ½ inch (with the exception of any joists or other blocking used for support).

Recessed downlights. Recessed downlights fall into two types: one comes prewired and grounded to its housing box; the other must be wired into a junction box previously nailed to a joist. Larger downlights may require the same type of support blocking described below for ceiling panels.

Before installing the downlight, you'll need to cut a hole for the fixture housing in the ceiling between two joists; in a suspended ceiling, simply remove one tile or panel.

Once you've determined the proper location, trace the outline of the fixture housing on the ceiling with a pencil; use a keyhole saw or saber saw to neatly cut the hole.

• **Downlight with box.** This type of fixture and its box are premounted on a metal frame (see drawing below). The unit is (A) first slipped through the hole cut in the ceiling and then (B) clipped to the ceiling's edge. Then the fixture housing (C) snaps into its socket.

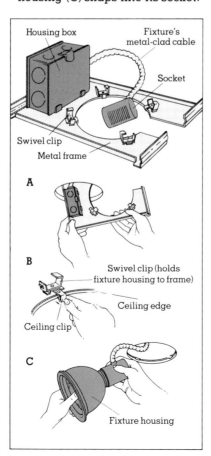

Housing box

Fixture's metal-clad cable

Socket

Swivel clip

Metal frame

A

B

Swivel clip (holds fixture housing to frame)

Ceiling edge

Ceiling clip

C

Fixture housing

• **Downlight without box.** To link this type of fixture with incoming cable, it's important to first select a junction box that can be nailed to a joist, as shown below. The fixture's metal-clad ("flex") cable is clamped and wired into the junction box. The fixture housing snaps into its socket, then the fixture is pushed into place and secured with clips to the ceiling material. The metal-clad cable grounds the fixture to the box.

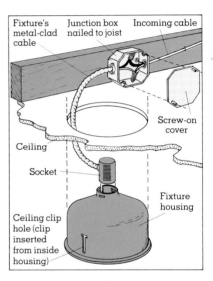

Fixture's metal-clad cable

Junction box nailed to joist

Incoming cable

Screw-on cover

Ceiling

Socket

Fixture housing

Ceiling clip hole (clip inserted from inside housing)

Recessed ceiling panels. Manufactured ceiling panels, or troffer units, are available in a range of sizes. Panels are often designed to fit exactly the space of a panel or tile in a suspended ceiling (see page 121). The fixture rests on the furring strips or metal channel that support the ceiling panels.

In a standard ceiling, you'll have to cut a hole between joists, build a support frame, and fasten the fixture to the frame. If you don't have access from the attic or crawlspace above, you may need to cut an oversize opening in the ceiling in order to install the support framing; you'll have to patch the ceiling later.

To prepare for the fixture, first mark its outline on the ceiling between two joists. (See page 99 for help in locating joists). Then, with a keyhole or saber saw, cut through the ceiling along the line and remove the material. Cut lengths of 2 by 4 scrap to fit snugly between adjacent joists. Nail the 2 by 4s flush with the bottoms of the joists, spaced to match the width or length of your fixture. Use extra blocking parallel to the joists as needed (see drawing below).

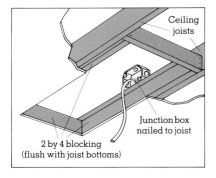

Ceiling joists

Junction box nailed to joist

2 by 4 blocking (flush with joist bottoms)

If your panel is wider than the space between adjacent joists, you'll need to cut away a portion of one joist and install headers to reinforce the gap. See "Skylight basics," page 103, for more details.

To provide electrical power, route cable to the ceiling panel from a junction box, switch box, or adjacent fixture box. The panel often has its own cover plate, or "box," to protect wire splices; if yours doesn't, nail a junction box nearby to house the connections.

If your only access is from below, connect the wiring to the panel before pushing the panel into the opening. Anchor the panel to the blocking or joists with nails, screws, or mounting hardware provided by the manufacturer.

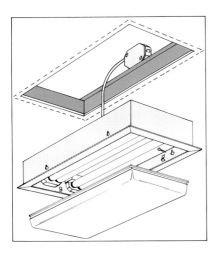

Installing dimmer switches

Most dimmer switches can be wired into existing circuits in the same way as the switches they replace. *(See page 110 for details on wiring switches.)* The one exception is a dimmer for a fluorescent fixture, which requires some added steps and hardware.

Incandescent dimmers. Usually a single switch controls a light or a group of lights. This type of switch is called a single-pole switch; it must be replaced with a single-pole dimmer.

Sometimes two switches control a light or group of lights, as at opposite ends of the kitchen. These are called three-way switches. If you want to add a dimmer to such a system, replace the three-way switch most frequently used with a three-way dimmer. Leave the second three-way switch in place.

Before installing a dimmer, make sure the power to the switch box is turned OFF. After you've unscrewed the switch plate and switch-mounting screws, pull the switch from its box. Detach the wires from the terminals on the switch and reattach them to similar terminals on the dimmer.

If the dimmer comes with short wires instead of terminals, use wirenuts to splice their free ends to the wires in the switch box. A typical three-way dimmer is shown below *(for details on using wirenuts, see page 110).*

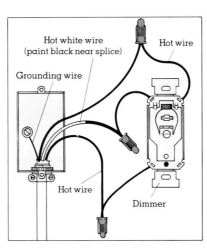

Hot white wire (paint black near splice)

Hot wire

Grounding wire

Hot wire

Dimmer

On three-way switches and dimmers, one of the terminals will be marked "common"; the wire attached to the common terminal on the switch is attached to the common terminal on the dimmer.

Fluorescent dimmers. If you're considering a dimmer for a fluorescent fixture, first make sure the fixture is equipped with rapid-start tubes; modern dimmers won't function with old-style preheat tubes. Then you must replace the ballast (transformer) in the fixture with a special dimming ballast. A typical wiring situation is shown below.

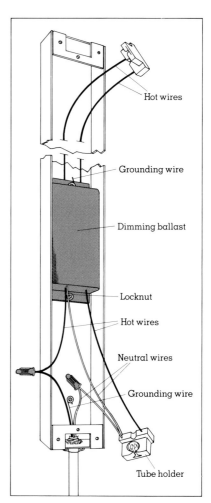

Hot wires

Grounding wire

Dimming ballast

Locknut

Hot wires

Neutral wires

Grounding wire

Tube holder

Use a dimming ballast with two hot wires and matching dimmer to avoid rewiring the run between them with five-wire cable—a difficult chore. Wire the two-wire fluorescent dimmer into the switch box as you would an incandescent dimmer.

UNDER-CABINET LIGHTING—A TASK FORCE

The constant demand for additional kitchen storage pays an unexpected dividend to homeowners searching for ways to light work centers. Make your cabinets and shelves do double duty: attach task lights underneath them to shed bright, even light over the sink, range, menu-planning center, or other areas requiring supplemental illumination.

Many types of incandescent and fluorescent fixtures—ready-made or for you to assemble—are available for installation beneath cabinets and shelves.

Fluorescent fixtures

A popular choice for task lighting, fluorescent fixtures spread a diffuse light that minimizes shadows. Their long, slender shapes and low operating temperatures make them ideal choices for under-cabinet installation. Fluorescent tubes are also twice as efficient as incandescent bulbs and last from five to ten times as long.

Fluorescent lights can be permanently wired into electric circuitry or plugged into nearby outlets. If each fixture is operated from its own switch, you'll have greatest control of the light and least waste of energy. Dimmers may be added to lower the intensity at times when only general illumination is required.

One of the most common types of fluorescent lighting, and one of the easiest to install, is an integral unit composed of one or two tubes and a ballast. For greatest efficiency, the fixture should span at least two-thirds of the area to be lighted and should be positioned as close as possible to the front of the cabinet.

Adding a wood or metal valance to a fixture mounted at eye level hides the unit and eliminates glare (see illustration below).

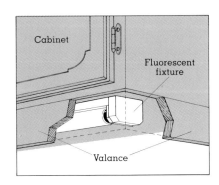

To build a valance to match your cabinet's decor, measure the required space and cut a piece of cardboard to use as a mockup.

For more flexibility, you can buy lengths of metal strip lights and join them to extend the light under a cabinet of any size. The strips are equipped with built-in valances in a choice of finishes. Besides accommodating fluorescent bulbs, the systems offer incandescent spotlight (see illustration below) and mini-light options.

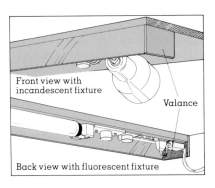

To install strips under wooden cabinets or shelves, simply screw them into the lower surface. Mounting clips easily attach a unit to glass shelves.

Incandescent alternatives

Incandescent task-lighting options include curio lights (similar to those mounted on picture frames), strip lighting to buy or build, and miniature track lights.

Incandescent bulbs can be plugged into the strip lighting unit mentioned above, or you can assemble your own components (see below). The two most common types of strips are plug-ins, with bulbs positioned in set locations, and parallel conductor strips, in which bulbs can be positioned all along the length of the strip.

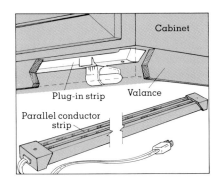

Miniature track lights (see illustration below) work just like their larger relatives. Installation is similar to that for strip lighting. Continuous electrical tracks allow you to position fixtures where you choose.

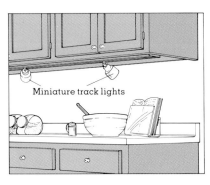

Walls & ceilings

Installing a new wall (see page 98) or a suspended ceiling can change the entire appearance of your room. Or you can give your kitchen a completely new look simply by splashing on a coat of colorful paint or by applying a complementary wall covering.

Even adding a new wall surface is relatively easy. Gypsum wallboard, the most popular choice, is inexpensive and provides a good surface for paint, wallpaper, tile, plastic laminate, or paneling.

Fortunately, these improvements are among the easiest projects for the average homeowner to tackle—many of the new products on the market require little or no experience to apply.

If your kitchen's ceiling is something you'd like to hide, a lightweight, trim solution might be to install a suspended ceiling with metal grid frame and fiberboard panels. Such a ceiling also permits easy installation of recessed light fixtures for both general and task lighting (see pages 114–115).

Installing gypsum wallboard

Cutting and installing gypsum wallboard is a straightforward procedure, but concealing the joints between panels and in the corners demands patience and care. And the weight of full panels can be awkward to negotiate. Wallboard is easily damaged; take care not to bend or break the corners or tear the paper covers.

Standard wallboard panels are 4 feet wide and from 8 feet to 16 feet long. Common thicknesses are ⅜ inch for a backing material for other wall coverings, ½ inch for final wall coverings, and ⅝ inch where the walls border a garage space. Choose water-resistant wallboard, identified by green or blue paper covers, in the sink area or wherever moisture might collect.

Cutting wallboard. To make a straight cut, first mark the cut line on the front paper layer with a pencil and straightedge, or snap a line with a chalkline. Cut through the front paper with a utility knife.

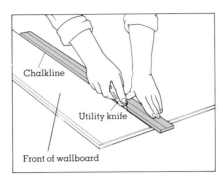

Chalkline

Utility knife

Front of wallboard

Turn the wallboard over and break the gypsum core by bending it toward the back. Finally, cut the back paper along the bend. Smooth the edge of the cut with a perforated rasp.

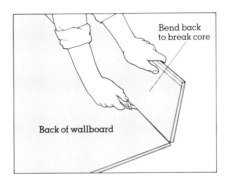

Bend back to break core

Back of wallboard

When fitting wallboard around obstructions such as doorways or electrical outlet boxes, carefully measure from the edge of an adjacent wallboard panel or reference point to the obstruction. Transfer the measurements to a new panel, and cut out the correct area. For openings within a panel, drill a pilot hole and make the cutout with a keyhole or wallboard saw. Larger edge cutouts should also be made with a keyhole or wallboard saw.

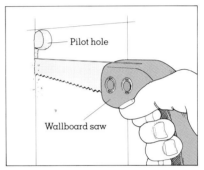

Pilot hole

Wallboard saw

Nailing the panels. Before installing panels, mark the stud locations on the floor and ceiling. Center the wallboard edges over two studs and fasten with wallboard nails. Drive in the nails with a hammer, dimpling the wallboard surface without puncturing the paper. Nail the panel to the inside studs. Nail spacing will be specified by local codes. Typical spacing is every 6 inches.

If your wallboard will serve as a backing for ceramic tile, paneling, or cabinets, you may not need to hide joints and corners. But if

HOW TO INSTALL GYPSUM WALLBOARD

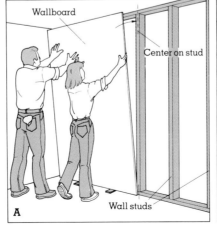

Wallboard

Center on stud

Wall studs

A

Space nails every 6 inches

B

Lift the wallboard panel into position (A) and center the edges over wall studs. Then nail the panel to the studs (B), dimpling the wallboard surface slightly with the hammer.

... Walls & ceilings

HOW TO TAPE WALLBOARD JOINTS

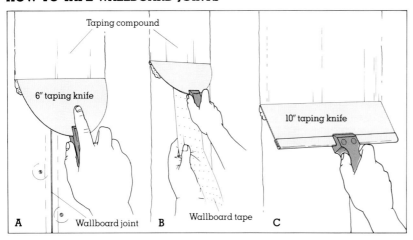

To tape a wallboard joint, spread a smooth layer of taping compound over the joint (A), embed paper tape in compound (B), and apply a second, thinner layer of compound. When it's dry, sand smooth and apply a wider layer (C), feathering the edges.

you're painting or wallpapering, you'll want to finish the wallboard.

Taping joints and corners. To finish wallboard neatly, you'll need wallboard tape (buy tape that's precreased) and taping compound.

The taping process is done in stages. To tape a joint between panels, first apply a smooth layer of taping compound over the joint with a 6-inch taping knife. Before the compound dries, embed wallboard tape into it and apply another thin coat of compound over the tape, smoothing it gently with the knife.

To tape an inside corner, apply a smooth layer of compound to the wallboard on each side of the corner. Measure and tear the tape, fold it in half vertically along the crease, and press it into the corner with a corner tool. Apply a thin layer of compound over the tape and smooth it out with the corner tool.

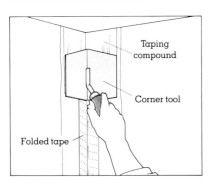

Exterior corners are covered with a protective metal cornerbead and finished with compound.

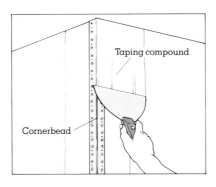

Continue taping all the joints. Then, using smooth, even strokes with the 6-inch knife, cover the inside nail dimples with compound.

Allow the taping compound to dry for at least 24 hours before sanding lightly to get a smooth surface. (NOTE: Wear a face mask and goggles while sanding.

Using a 10-inch knife, apply a second coat of compound, feathering out the edges past each side of the taped joint.

Let the second coat dry. Then sand it and apply a final coat. Use a 10-inch or an even wider knife to smooth out and feather the edges, covering all dimples and joints. After the compound dries, sand it again to remove even minor imperfections.

Painting your kitchen

A fresh coat of paint provides the fastest way to "remodel" your kitchen. Below are some guidelines to help you do a good job.

Choosing the paint. Your basic choices in paint are latex (waterbase) paint (also called acrylic or vinyl) and oil-base paint.

Tools of the trade. Choosing the correct brushes is almost as important as selecting the paint.

• **Natural bristles** (hog hairs) are traditionally used to apply oil-base paints. They should not be used with latex paint; the bristles soak up water from the paint and quickly become soggy and useless.

• **Synthetic bristles,** nylon or nylon-like, are best for applying latex, but most can also be used with oil-base paints.

What size brush do you need? For window sashes, shutters, and trim, choose a 1½ or 2-inch angled sash brush. For woodwork and other medium-size surfaces, a 2 or 3-inch brush is best. And for walls, ceilings, and most paneling, choose a 3½ or 4-inch brush—if brushing is your choice.

When you want to paint a large flat area quickly and easily, though, a roller is the answer. A 9-inch roller will handle all interior paint jobs. A handle threaded to accommodate an extension pole will allow you to reach high walls and ceilings without a ladder or scaffolding. The roller's cover, like paint brush bristles, is important—choose a nylon blend for latex, lambskin for oil-base paint, or a mohair cover for use with both. A well-designed roller tray is also essential.

A pad applicator, which resembles a sponge attached to a short handle, is handy for clean edging and for use in tight spots.

Preparing the surface. A key factor in preventing cracking and peeling after the paint dries is preparing the

TOOLS OF THE PAINTING TRADE

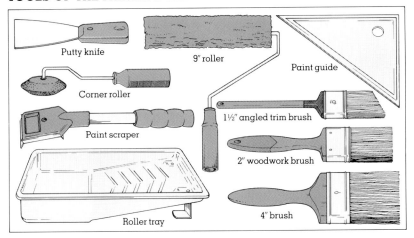

Putty knife

9″ roller

Paint guide

Corner roller

1½″ angled trim brush

Paint scraper

2″ woodwork brush

4″ brush

Roller tray

surface correctly. It's *essential* to the bonding and durability of any latex paint application.

Start by removing light fixtures and faceplates. Then inspect the area you're painting for small holes as well as more extensive damage, and make all necessary repairs.

If an old paint finish is flaking, you must sand it smooth. And when you paint over a glossy surface, you must first roughen the old finish with sandpaper so the new paint will adhere. Use a sponge soaked with paint thinner on any spots that are very greasy. Then an overall dusting, a sponging with an abrasive cleanser, and rinsing (complete a small area at a time) will finish off the surface preparation. Allow about 24 hours for all washed areas to dry completely.

Sometimes an old finish is in such poor condition that the paint must be removed entirely. The easiest method of stripping old paint is to apply a commercial liquid paint remover, then scrape off the softened paint with a broad knife or paint scraper. Finish the surface by sanding lightly until it's clean and smooth.

It's possible to paint over wallpaper that's smooth and attached firmly to the wall. Apply a sealing primer such as pigmented shellac or a flat oil-base enamel undercoat. Let the sealer dry completely before you paint.

It's often safer, though, to re-move the wallpaper, especially if it's tearing and flaking. See "Hanging new wallpaper" for details.

Unpainted plaster or wallboard should be primed with latex paint or latex primer-sealer. Prime unpainted wood with oil-base paint whether you plan to finish with oil-base or latex.

Painting tips. If you're painting both walls and ceiling, start with the ceiling. Paint the entire ceiling without stopping. You'll want to paint in rectangles, approximately 2 feet by 3 feet, starting in a corner and working across the ceiling in the direction of the shortest distance.

Begin the first section by using a brush, pad applicator, or special corner roller to paint a narrow strip next to the wall line and around any fixtures. Then finish the section with a roller, overlapping any brush marks. Continue painting, one section at a time, from one end of the ceiling to the other and back again.

Then it's on to the walls. Mentally divide a wall into 3-foot-square sections, starting from a corner at the ceiling line and working down the wall. As with ceilings, use a brush, pad applicator, or corner roller along the ceiling line, corners, fixtures, or edges of openings. Finish each section with a roller, overlapping any brush marks.

At the bottom edge along the floor or baseboard, or along the edges of cabinets and counters, use a brush and paint guide; as before, overlap the brush strokes with a roller. Return to the ceiling line and again work down in 3-foot sections.

Hanging new wallpaper

Next to paint, wallpaper is the most popular covering for kitchen walls. Easier than ever to install, wallpaper is available in a kaleidoscope of colors and patterns.

Choices for the kitchen. A wallpaper for the kitchen should be scrubbable, durable, and stain resistant. *Solid vinyl* wallpapers, available in a wide variety of colors and textures, fill the bill. *Vinyl coatings* also give wallpaper a washable surface but aren't notably durable or grease resistant.

If you're a beginner, you may want to consider prepasted and pretrimmed paper.

To find an adhesive suitable for your material, check the manufacturer's instructions or ask your dealer.

Preparing the surface. To prepare for papering, you'll need to remove all light fixtures and faceplates. Thoroughly clean and rinse the surface. Most manufacturers recommend that you completely remove any old wallpaper before hanging a nonporous covering like solid vinyl.

If the existing paper is strippable, it will come off easily when you pull it up at a corner or seam. To remove nonstrippable wallpaper, use either a steamer (available for rent from your dealer) or a spray bottle filled with very hot water. Before steaming, break the surface of the old paper by sanding it with very coarse sandpaper or by pulling a sawblade sideways across the wall.

Within a few minutes of steaming (wait longer if it's a nonporous material), you can begin to remove the old paper. Using a broad knife, work down from the top of the wall, scraping off the old wallpaper.

If yours is a new gypsum wallboard surface, tape all joints between panels (see page 118) before papering. When dry, sand the wall

... Walls & ceilings

smooth and apply a coat of flat, oil-base primer-sealer.

If you want to apply wallpaper over previously painted surfaces that are in good condition, simply clean off all the dirt, grease, and oil, and let it dry. If latex paint was used, or if you can't determine the type, you must apply an oil-base undercoat over the old paint.

Ready to start? Plan the best place to hang your first strip. If you're papering all four walls with a patterned paper, the last strip you hang probably won't match the first, so plan to start and finish in the least conspicuous place—usually a corner, door casing, or window casing.

Most house walls are not straight and plumb, so you'll need to establish a plumb line. Figure the width of your first strip of wallpaper minus ½ inch (which will overlap the corner or casing); measure that distance from your starting point, and mark the wall. Using a carpenter's level as a straightedge, draw a line through your mark that's perfectly plumb. Extend the line until it reaches from floor to ceiling.

It's a good idea to measure the wall height before cutting each strip of wallpaper. Allow 2 inches extra at the top and bottom. Be sure also to allow for pattern match.

Using a razor knife, cut the strips. Number them on the back at the top edge so you can apply them in the proper sequence.

With some wallpapers, you'll need to spread adhesive on the backing with a wide, soft paint roller or pasting brush; other papers are prepasted—all you have to do is soak them in water before hanging.

After pasting or soaking, strips should be "booked," as shown below, until ready to hang.

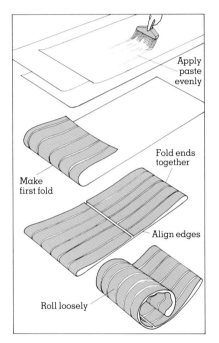

Apply paste evenly

Make first fold

Fold ends together

Align edges

Roll loosely

Trim the edges of the wallpaper at this stage, if necessary. You're now ready to hang the paper.

Hanging the wallpaper. First, position a stepladder next to the plumb line you've marked. Open the top fold of the first booked strip, raising it so that it overlaps the ceiling line by 2 inches. Carefully align the strip's edge with the plumb line.

Using a smoothing brush, press the strip against the wall. Smooth out all wrinkles and air bubbles. Then release the lower portion of the strip and smooth it into place.

Carefully roll the edges flat, if necessary, with a seam roller. To trim along the ceiling and baseboard, use a broad knife and a very sharp razor knife. With a sponge dipped in lukewarm water, remove any excess adhesive before it dries.

Unfold your second strip on the wall in the same way you did the first. Gently butt the second strip against the first, aligning the pattern as you move down the wall. Continue around the room with the remaining paper.

Dealing with corners. Because few rooms have perfectly straight corners, you'll have to measure from the edge of the preceding strip to the corner; do this at three heights.

HANGING THE FIRST STRIP

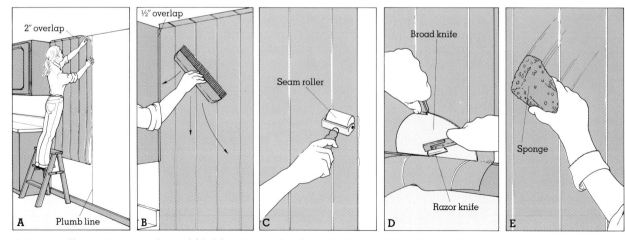

2" overlap

½" overlap

Seam roller

Broad knife

Razor knife

Sponge

A   Plumb line   B   C   D   E

To hang wallpaper, first open the top fold of the strip, overlap the ceiling line, and align the strip's edge with the plumb line (A); press the strip against the wall with a smoothing brush (B). Release the lower fold and smooth into place; roll the edges flat with a seam roller (C). Trim the strip along the ceiling and baseboard with a broad knife and a razor knife (D). Remove excess adhesive with a sponge dipped in lukewarm water (E).

Cut a strip ½ inch wider than the widest measurement. Butting the strip to the preceding strip, brush it firmly into and around the corner. At the top and bottom corners, cut the overlap so the strip will lie flat.

Next, measure the width of the leftover piece of wallpaper. On the adjacent wall, measure the same distance from the corner and make a plumb line at that point.

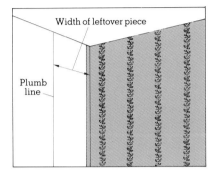

Position one edge of the strip along the plumb line; the other edge will cover the ½-inch overlap. (If you're hanging vinyl wallpaper, you should apply a vinyl-to-vinyl adhesive on top of the overlap.)

Cutouts. It's easy to cut around electrical switches and plug-in outlets. Be sure all faceplates have been removed before hanging the wallpaper; then before making the cutout, shut off the electricity.

Hang the paper as described above. Then use a razor knife to make an X-shaped cut over the opening, extending the cuts to each corner. Trim the excess along the edges of the opening with the razor knife and a broad knife.

Installing a suspended ceiling

Easy-to-install suspended ceilings consist of a metal grid suspended from above with wire or spring-type hangers. The grid holds acoustic or decorative fiberboard panels.

The most common panel size is 2 feet by 4 feet, though panels are available in a variety of sizes. Transparent and translucent panels and egg-crate grilles are made to fit the gridwork to admit light from

HOW TO INSTALL A SUSPENDED CEILING

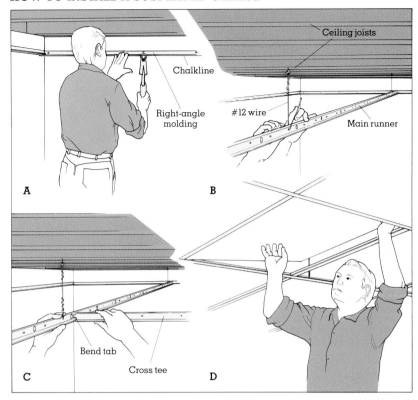

To hang a suspended ceiling, snap a chalkline around the room and install L-shaped molding with its base on the chalkline (A). Set the main runners on the molding at each end, attach them to the joists with #12 wire (B), lock 4-foot cross tees to the main runners (C), and push the panels into place (D).

above. Recessed lighting panels that exactly replace one panel also are available from some manufacturers. All components are replaceable, and the panels can be raised for access to the area above.

Figuring your needs. Here is the easiest way to determine the number of panels you'll need: Measure your wall lengths at the proposed ceiling height. Draw the ceiling area to scale on graph paper, using one square per foot of ceiling size. Block in the panel size you'll be using. Finally, count the blocked areas and parts of areas to get the number of panels you'll need.

For a professional-looking job, plan equal borders on the opposite sides of the room. To determine the nonstandard width of panels needed for perimeter rows, measure the extra space from the last full row of panels to one wall and divide by two. This final figure will be the

dimension of border tiles against that wall and the opposite wall. Repeat this procedure for the other room dimensions.

Installing the ceiling. First, figure the ceiling height—at least 3 inches below plumbing, 5 inches below lights (minimum ceiling height is 7 feet 6 inches). Snap a chalkline around the room at that level and install L-shaped angle molding with its base on the chalkline.

Next, install the main runners perpendicular to the ceiling joists, (see above). Cut the runners to length with tinsnips. Setting them on the molding at each end, support them every 4 feet with #12 wire attached to small eyebolts screwed into joists above. Lock 4-foot cross tees to the main runners by bending the tabs in the runner spots.

Set the panels into place and install any recessed lighting panels. Cut border panels as necessary.

Cabinets & countertops

Installing new cabinets and dressing them up with the countertops of your choice can be the passport to a whole new world of kitchen style and efficiency.

Removing and installing cabinets and countertops is not difficult and requires only basic hand tools. But the work must be done carefully to ensure a professional-looking fit.

Removing old cabinets

If you remove base cabinets first, you'll have room to get underneath wall cabinets without strain, and you'll avoid damaging walls or cabinets.

Base cabinets. First, pry away any vinyl wall base, floor covering, or molding from the base cabinet's kickspace or sides, as shown above. Next, disconnect plumbing supply lines and the drain trap from the kitchen sink *(see page 135)*. Also disconnect plumbing and electrical lines to a dishwasher or garbage disposer *(see page 136)*, electric or gas range, wall ovens, or cooktop *(see pages 139–140)*. *Be sure plumbing and gas lines and electrical circuits are properly shut off before disconnecting them.* Remove the sink, fixtures, and appliances from the area.

Old base cabinets are usually attached to wall studs with screws or nails through nailing strips at the back of each unit. Sometimes they're also fastened to the floor with nails through the kickspace trim or cabinet sides. Screws are easy to remove unless they're old and stripped. To remove nails, you may need to pry the cabinet away from the wall or floor with a pry bar (use a wood scrap between the pry bar and the wall or floor to prevent damaging those surfaces).

Several base units may be fastened together and covered with a single countertop. If you can remove the entire assembly intact, you'll save time and labor. Otherwise, unscrew or pry the units apart—they're fastened either through adjacent sides or face frames—and remove the countertop.

CABINET ANATOMY

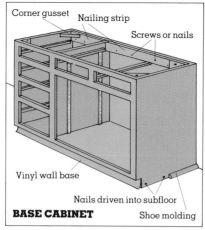

BASE CABINET

Labels: Corner gusset · Nailing strip · Screws or nails · Vinyl wall base · Nails driven into subfloor · Shoe molding

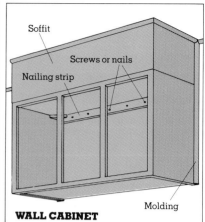

WALL CABINET

Labels: Soffit · Screws or nails · Nailing strip · Molding

Countertops typically are anchored to the cabinet frame from below, through rails or corner gussets. Plastic laminate, hardwood butcherblock, and the backing for ceramic tile countertops are normally fastened with screws; masonry and synthetic marble are attached with adhesive.

Wall cabinets. Once the base cabinets are out of the way, you're ready to remove the wall cabinets. They're either screwed, bolted, or nailed through nailing strips at the back of the cabinets to wall studs behind each unit. They might also be fastened to the ceiling or an overhead soffit.

If the cabinets are screwed or bolted to the wall, recruit some helpers to hold them in place while you unfasten them. Then remove the cabinets from the area. If the cabinets are fastened with nails, you'll have to use a pry bar. Again, individual units are probably fastened together. If you have a helper or two, the assembly can often be removed intact.

Installing new cabinets

Both wall and base cabinets are carefully aligned with layout marks previously drawn on the walls. Then they're fastened to the wall studs with screws. In order to give yourself adequate working room, and prevent damage to base cabinets, it's best to install wall cabinets first.

Wall cabinets. Your first task is to locate and mark wall studs in the area of your new cabinets. *(For help in finding studs, see page 99.)* Snap a chalkline to mark the studs' centers, or draw lines with a soft pencil.

Next you'll need to lay out lines on the wall for the top and bottom of the cabinets. Measure up 84 inches from the floor (the standard top height for wall cabinets). Because floors are seldom completely level, measure in several spots and use the highest mark as your reference point. Trace a line from this mark across the wall, using a carpenter's level as a straightedge.

Now subtract the exact height of the new cabinet units from the top line, and draw this line on the wall. Tack a temporary ledger strip made from 1 by 2 or 2 by 4 lumber to the wall studs, with the ledger's top edge exactly flush with the bottom line.

Start your cabinet installation either from a corner of the kitchen or from the edge of the first cabinet. You can determine the location of the latter from your kitchen plans. Again, mark the wall.

Remove cabinet doors by their hinge pins, if possible. Then, with as much help as you can recruit, lift the first cabinet into place atop the ledger strip. While your helpers hold the cabinet in position, drill pilot holes through the top and bottom nailing strips and into wall studs; *loosely* fasten the cabinet to the studs with woodscrews long enough to

HOW TO MARK REFERENCE LINES

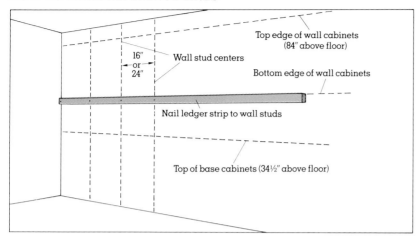

Top edge of wall cabinets (84" above floor)

16" or 24" — Wall stud centers

Bottom edge of wall cabinets

Nail ledger strip to wall studs

Top of base cabinets (34½" above floor)

extend 1½ inches into the studs when tight.

At this point, some careful attention to detail will ensure a first-rate installation. Check the cabinet carefully for level and plumb—from top to bottom and from front to back—with your carpenter's level. Because walls seldom are exactly plumb, you may have to make some fine adjustments to enable the cabinet to hang correctly. Bumps and high points on the wall can sometimes be sanded down; low points will need to be shimmed.

Drive shims as needed between the cabinet back and the wall, either down from the top or up from the bottom (in which case you'll need to remove the ledger strip). Tap the shims in a little at a time, and keep checking with the level. When all is in order, tighten the woodscrews; then recheck with the level. If the tightening has thrown the cabinet out of plumb, shim again.

Some cabinets are designed with "scribing strips" along the sides—extra material you can shave down to achieve a perfect fit between the cabinet and an irregular wall. To scribe a cabinet, first position it; then run a length of masking tape down the side to be scribed. Setting the points of a compass with pencil to the widest gap between the scribing strip and the wall, run the compass pivot down the wall next to the strip, as shown above right. The wall's irregularities will

be marked on the tape. Remove the cabinet from the wall, and use a block plane, file, or power belt sander to trim the scribing strip to the line. Then reinstall the cabinet.

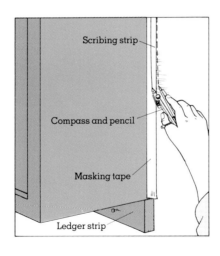

Scribing strip

Compass and pencil

Masking tape

Ledger strip

If your cabinets don't have scribing strips, you can cover any large irregularities with decorative molding or latex caulk.

Adjacent wall cabinets may be joined together on the wall or on the floor; clamp them together with C-clamps, carefully align the front edges, and screw together adjacent cabinet sides or face frames, as shown at right.

Base cabinets. Though base cabinets are less awkward to position than wall cabinets, you must now deal with the vagaries of both wall and floor.

Before you begin, remove any baseboard, moldings, or wall base that might interfere. From the floor, measure up 34½ inches—the height of a standard base cabinet.

Again, take several measurements and use the highest mark for your reference point. Draw a level line through the mark and across the wall.

If you need to cut access holes in a cabinet's back or bottom for plumbing supply and drain pipes, or for electrical wire serving the sink complex, you'll want to do so *before* you install the cabinet.

With helpers, move the cabinet into position, threading any plumbing connections or wiring through the access holes. Measure the cabinet carefully for level and plumb—from side to side and front to back. Then shim the unit as necessary between the cabinet base and floor.

Scribing strips may be included along the sides to allow full alignment with the wall. Both shims and irregularities in the floor can be hidden by baseboard trim, vinyl wall base, or new flooring.

When the cabinet is aligned, drill pilot holes through the nailing strip at the back of the cabinet into the wall studs. Fasten the unit to the studs with woodscrews.

Once installed, base cabinets are fastened together like wall cabinets: screw together the adjacent sides or face frames. Now it's time to install the new countertop; for instructions, see pages 125–127.

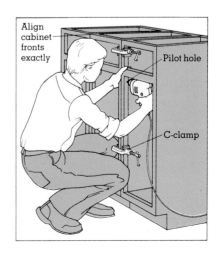

Align cabinet fronts exactly

Pilot hole

C-clamp

TIPS FOR PATCHING WALLBOARD & PLASTER

Sometimes, all it takes to add new life to kitchen walls are a few repairs and a fresh coat of paint. Gypsum wallboard and plaster, the two most common wall materials, are not difficult to patch, but you'll have to work carefully to match the patch to the surrounding surface.

Patching gypsum wallboard

Cracks, nail holes, or gouge marks can be patched with a putty knife and either spackling compound or patching plaster; cracks may also be filled with a special crack patcher.

To patch holes between wall studs, first cut a neat rectangle around the hole with a sharp utility knife or hacksaw blade. Then, from another piece of wallboard, cut a rectangle 1 inch larger on all sides. Laying the new piece face side down, recut it the same size as the wall rectangle—*without* scoring the paper on the face side. Lift off the inch of cut board around all sides, leaving the paper margins intact (A).

Spread a thin layer of spackling compound around and on the edges of the hole. Position the patch (B) and cover the seams and entire surface with a thin coating of spackle. Let it dry; then smooth carefully with fine sandpaper.

Large holes will normally uncover at least one wall stud, which may be used as a nailing surface for the new patch. Or you can enlarge the hole to use two flanking studs as nailing surfaces. For best support, nail the patch to horizontal blocking installed between the studs. Install, and finish the patch as if you were installing a brand new panel *(see pages 117–118 for techniques)*.

Patching plaster walls

Small cracks in plaster are treated exactly like those in wallboard, except that extra steps may be required to match the present surface texture (see below).

For holes or wide cracks that go all the way to the lath or wallboard backing, first knock out all loose, cracked plaster with a hammer and chisel. Undercut the edges to strengthen the eventual bond. Using a sponge, dampen the area surrounding the hole.

If the hole is larger than 4 inches square, it will take three layers to fill. The first layer should fill a little more than half the depth and should bond to the lath backing (A). Before this layer dries (about 4 hours), score it with a nail (B) to provide a "bite" for succeeding layers.

Re-wet the dried patch and apply a second layer. This coat should come within ½ inch to ¼ inch of the surface. Again, let the patching plaster dry; then apply the third coat.

To fill deep holes without backing (for example, where an electrical housing box has been removed), first pry out any cracked material around the hole and dust the area thoroughly. Then loop a length of wire through a piece of rust-resistant screen, as shown below. Push the screen through the hole to be filled, and wind it tightly back against the wall with the wire and a stick (A). Wet the wall adjacent to the hole, and fill the hole with patching plaster to half its depth (B). When the patch is dry, cut off the wire and finish filling the hole.

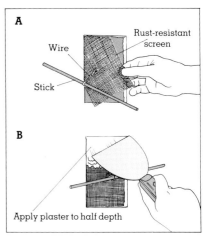

A
Wire
Rust-resistant screen
Stick
B
Apply plaster to half depth

Matching an existing texture requires special treatment of the still-wet plaster. For a smooth surface, pull a wide putty knife or a rubber float across the surface; to achieve an almost glossy smoothness, wipe the plaster with a wet sponge held in one hand, just ahead of the float in the other hand. For a rough surface, scour lightly with a paint brush—either in swirling strokes or jabbed straight at the wall, depending on the texture you're matching.

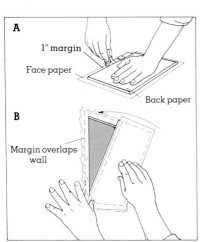

A
1" margin
Face paper
Back paper
B
Margin overlaps wall

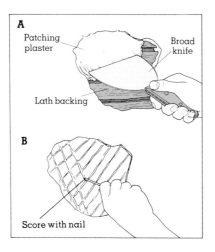

A
Patching plaster
Broad knife
Lath backing
B
Score with nail

... Cabinets & countertops

Installing plastic laminate countertops

Plastic laminate countertops, by far the most common countertops used in kitchens, are divided into two types: post-formed and self-rimmed *(for self-rimmed, see page 126)*.

Post-formed countertops are premolded one-piece tops, from curved backsplash to bullnosed front. They're available in several standard lengths (usually from 6 to 12 feet) and can be cut to the exact length you need. Most types are offered with accessory kits for endsplashes (where the countertop meets a side wall or cabinet) and endcaps.

The term "self-rimmed" simply means that you apply the laminate of your choice over an old countertop or new core material. Though post-formed countertops are simpler to install, building your own enables you to choose from a much greater selection of laminates. You can also tailor the dimensions of the backsplash, endsplash, and overhang to your exact requirements.

Post-formed countertop. Since post-formed countertops come only in standard sizes, you'll normally need to buy one slightly larger than you need and cut it to length. To cut the countertop with a handsaw, mark the cut line on the face. Mark the back if you're using a power saw. Use masking tape to protect the cutting line against chipping (you'll probably have to draw the line again, this time on the tape). Smooth the edge of the cut with a file or sandpaper. Plan to cover that end with an endcap or endsplash.

Exactly what size do you need? The standard overhang on a laminate top varies between ¾ inch and 1 inch in front and on open ends. Add these dimensions to the dimensions of your cabinet. If you plan to include an endsplash at one or both ends, check the endsplash kit: since most endsplashes are assembled directly above the end of the cabinet, you generally *subtract* ¾ inch from the length of the countertop on that side.

POST-FORMED LAMINATE COUNTERTOP

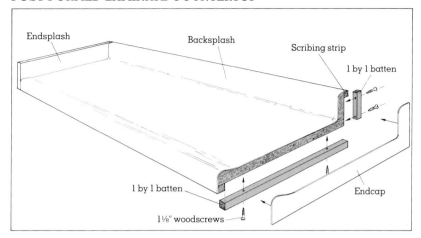

Endsplashes are screwed either directly into the edge of the countertop or into "built-down" wood battens previously attached to the edge, as shown above. Apply silicone sealant to the surfaces to be joined. Holding the endsplash in place with C-clamps, drill pilot holes if needed and drive in the screws.

Endcaps (preshaped strips of matching laminate) are glued to an open end with contact cement or, in some cases, pressed into place with a hot iron. Again, you first may need to build down the edge with wood battens. File the edges of the new strip flush with the top and front edges of the countertop, or use an electric router and laminate-trimming bit.

If your cabinets are U-shaped or L-shaped, you'll need to buy mitered countertop sections or have them cut to order. (It's very difficult to cut accurate miters at home.) The mitered sections should have small slots along the bottom edges. They are connected with take-up or draw bolts, as shown below. Coat the

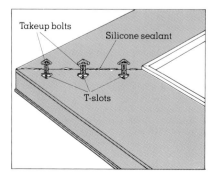

edges with silicone sealant, align the edges carefully, and tighten the bolts. Fasten the adjoining backsplashes together with woodscrews.

Countertops, like cabinets, rarely fit uniformly against the back or side walls because the walls rarely are straight. Usually the back edge of a post-formed countertop comes with a scribing strip that can be trimmed to follow the exact contours of the wall. Follow the instructions for scribing cabinets, detailed on page 123.

Position the countertop on the cabinet frame. Carefully check with a level—across the front and from front to back. Also make sure you can freely open and close the cabinet doors and top drawers with the countertop overhang in place. You may need to add shims or wood blocks around the perimeter and along cross-members of the cabinet top to level or raise the surface.

Fasten the countertop to the cabinets by running screws from below through the cabinet corner gussets or top frame *(see drawing, page 122)* and through any shims or wood blocks. Use woodscrews just long enough to penetrate ½ inch into the countertop core. Run a bead of silicone sealant along all exposed seams between the countertop and walls; clean up any excess.

If you need to cut a hole for a sink or cooktop in the new countertop, you'll need a keyhole or saber saw, and a drill for pilot holes. See page 135 for more details.

(Continued on next page)

... Cabinets & countertops

SELF-RIMMED LAMINATE COUNTERTOP

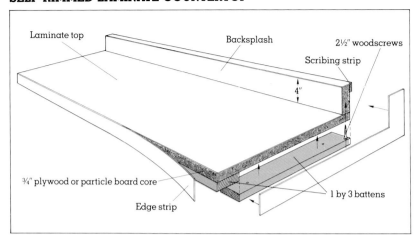

Laminate top · Backsplash · 2½" woodscrews · Scribing strip · 4" · ¾" plywood or particle board core · Edge strip · 1 by 3 battens

Self-rimmed laminate countertop. To build your own laminate countertop, you'll need to choose the laminate (¹/₁₆-inch thickness is the standard) and cut the core material to size from ¾-inch plywood or high-density particle board.

Build down the edges of the core with 1 by 3 battens (see drawing above). Then proceed to laminate the countertop. Do sides and front strips first, then the top surface, in the following manner:

Measure each surface to be laminated, adding ¼ inch to all dimensions as a margin for error. Mark the cutting line. Score the line with a sharp utility knife; then cut with a fine-toothed saw (face up with a handsaw, face down with a power saw). A laminate cutter is ideal.

Apply contact cement to both the laminate back and core surface to be joined, and allow the cement to dry for 20 to 30 minutes. Carefully check alignment before joining the two; once joined, the laminate can't be moved. Press the laminate into place, using a roller or a rolling pin to ensure even contact.

Use a block plane to trim the laminate flush with the core's edges; then dress it with a file. Or trim with an electric router equipped with a laminate-trimming bit.

Backsplashes or endsplashes should be cut from the same core material as the main countertop, then butt-joined to the countertop with sealant and woodscrews.

Installing ceramic tile countertops

Wall tiles, lighter and thinner than floor tiles, are the normal choice for countertops and backsplashes. Standard sizes range from 3 inches by 3 inches to 4½ inches by 8½ inches, with thicknesses varying from ¼ inch to ⅜ inch.

Preparing the base. Before you can lay tile, it's best to remove any present countertops (see page 122); then install ¾-inch exterior plywood, cut flush with the cabinet top, by screwing it to the cabinet frame from below.

Both the plywood base and the wall surface may need to be primed or sealed before tile is applied. To determine whether you need to prime or seal, read the information on the

adhesive container or ask your supplier.

Planning your layout. Before you start laying tile, you must decide how you want to trim the countertop edge and the sink. For ideas, see the drawing below.

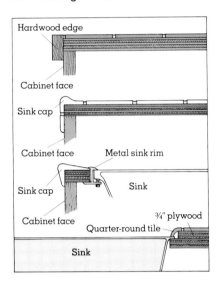

Hardwood edge · Cabinet face · Sink cap · Cabinet face · Metal sink rim · Sink cap · Sink · Cabinet face · ¾" plywood · Quarter-round tile · Sink

If you decide to use wood trim, seal the wood and attach it to the cabinet face with finishing nails. When in place, the wood strip's top edge should be positioned at the same height as the finished tile. A recessed sink, commonly used with tile countertops, is also installed at this time (see page 135).

On the front edge of your plywood base, locate and mark the point where the center of the sink or the

HOW TO SET COUNTERTOP TILES

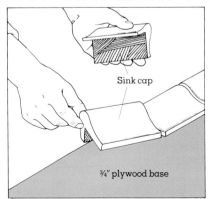

Sink cap · ¾" plywood base

First, set edge tiles in place, starting from the center line, after buttering the backs with adhesive.

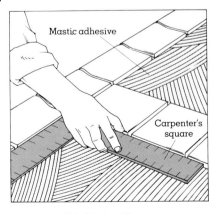

Mastic adhesive · Carpenter's square

Next, install field tiles. Use a square to keep the tiles perpendicular to the edge trim.

midpoint of a blank countertop will be. Lay the edge tiles out on the countertop, starting from your mark. Some tiles have small ceramic lugs molded onto their edges to keep spacing equal; if your tiles don't, use plastic spacers, available from your tile supplier.

Carefully position the rest of the "field" tiles on the countertop. Observing the layout, make any necessary adjustments to eliminate narrow cuts or difficult fits.

If the countertop will have a backsplash or will turn a corner, be sure to figure the cove or corner tiles into your layout.

Mark reference points of your layout on the plywood base to help you re-create it later; then remove the tile.

Setting the tiles. Set all trim tiles before spreading adhesive for the field tiles. Type I mastic, water-resistant and easy to use, is the best adhesive choice for countertops.

Butter the back of each front-edge tile and press into place, aligning it with the reference marks. If your edge trim consists of two tile rows, set the vertical piece first.

Next, butter any back cove tiles and set them against the wall. If you've installed a recessed sink, next lay the sink trim. Be sure to caulk between the sink and the base before setting the trim. If you're using quarter-round trim, you can either

miter the corners or use special corner pieces available with some patterns.

Next, spread adhesive over a section of the countertop (for tools and techniques, see page 130). Begin laying the field tiles, working from front to back. Cut tiles to fit, as necessary. As you lay the tiles, check the alignment frequently with a carpenter's square.

To set the tiles and level their faces, slide a 1-foot-square scrap of cloth-covered plywood over them and tap the scrap with a hammer.

Now set the backsplash, beginning one grout joint space above the cove tiles or countertop tiles. Cover the backsplash area with adhesive; for a better grip, you can also butter the back of each tile.

Unless you're tiling up to an overhead cabinet or window sill, use bullnose tiles for the last row. If a wall contains electrical switches or plug-in outlets, you can cut tiles in two and use tile nippers to nip out a hole.

Applying the grout. Remove any spacers, and clean the tile surface and grout joints until they're free of adhesive. Allow mastic adhesive to set for 24 hours before grouting the joints. For details on grouting tools and techniques, see page 131.

After grouting, wait at least 2 weeks for the grout to cure; then apply a recommended sealer.

Installing synthetic marble countertops

Some types of synthetic marble can be cut, shaped, and joined using woodworking techniques, though you will need power tools and carbide-tipped blades to do the job well.

Synthetic marble used for countertops usually ranges from ½ inch to ¾ inch thick. The ½-inch thickness must be continuously supported by the cabinet frame or by closely spaced plywood blocks. If you're installing a sink, you should add cross-members to the cabinet frame for support.

When you cut the slab, be sure it is firmly supported throughout its length. Mark and cut on the back side. Protect the cutting line with masking tape.

The countertop can be edged with wood trim, strips of synthetic marble, or a combination. If you're skilled with an electric router, you can shape a variety of custom edge treatments in the marble. Be sure to apply petroleum jelly to adjacent surfaces to guard against scratches.

Both wood and marble edges and backsplashes are glued and clamped in place until dry. When joining wood to marble, use neoprene adhesive; for marble-to-marble joints, use an adhesive recommended by the manufacturer.

Before installing the countertop, run a bead of neoprene adhesive around the top of the cabinet frame and on top of any cross-members or plywood blocks. With helpers, lower the countertop into place, and press down to seat it in the adhesive. Apply silicone sealant between the countertop and walls.

HOW TO SET BACKSPLASH TILES

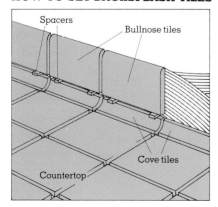

Align joints of backsplash tiles with tiles on the countertop; finish the top with bullnose tiles.

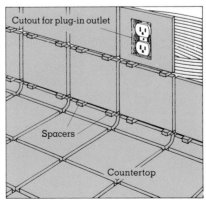

To fit tiles around plug-in outlets, cut a hole in the tile or cut the tile in two and nibble out a hole.

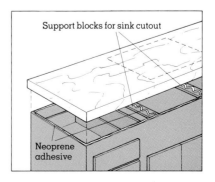

Flooring

Flooring manufacturers are continually revising their wares—improving selection, and making floors easier to care for and easier to install.

Two primary requirements for a kitchen floor are moisture-resistance and durability. Resilient sheet flooring, ceramic tile, and properly sealed hardwood strips all make good choices. Resilient flooring is the simplest of the three to install, especially if this is the only kitchen improvement you're planning. Ideally, both ceramic tile and hardwood strip floors are installed when cabinets, countertops, fixtures, doors, and appliances are not in the room.

The information in this section applies to floors supported by a standard subfloor, with joists or beams below (see drawing, page 97). If you're working with a cement slab, you may have to make special preparations to ensure that it's dry. For specific instructions, see the Sunset book Do-It-Yourself Flooring.

Resilient sheet flooring

Resilient sheet flooring can be laid in adhesive or placed loosely on the floor like wall-to-wall carpet. Though a few types are available in widths up to 12 feet, most sheet flooring is 6 feet wide and may require seaming.

Preparing the subfloor. Old resilient floors and wood floors both make acceptable bases for new resilient sheets, provided their surfaces are completely smooth and level. Old resilient flooring must be the solid not the cushioned type, and firmly bonded to the subfloor. Uneven wood floors may need a rough sanding (see page 133). Both types must be thoroughly cleaned, with loose tiles or boards secured in place.

Old flooring in poor condition or flooring of ceramic tile or masonry should be removed, if possible, down to the subfloor.

If it is impossible to remove without damaging the subfloor, or if the subfloor is in poor condition, cover the old flooring with ¼-inch underlayment-grade plywood, untempered hardboard, or particle board. Leave a ¹⁄₁₆-inch gap between panels to allow for later expansion. Fasten the panels down with 3-penny ring-shank or 4-penny cement-coated nails spaced 3 inches apart along the edges and 6 inches apart across the face of each panel.

Planning the new floor. Take exact measurements of the kitchen floor, and make a scale drawing on graph paper. Include the locations of any irregularities in the room: base cabinets, island cabinets, closets, or pantries. If your room is very irregular, you may want to make a full-size paper pattern of the floor instead of the scale drawing.

To cover a large area, it may be necessary to make a seam between two pieces. Looking at your floor plan or pattern, determine how to combine sheets so you can cover the floor with the minimum amount of material. If the flooring is patterned, you'll need enough extra to match the pattern at the seams.

Installing flooring without seams. The most critical step in laying sheet flooring is making the first rough cuts accurately.

Unroll the flooring in a large room or in a clean garage or basement. Transfer the floor plan—or paper pattern—directly onto the top of the flooring, using chalk or a water-soluble felt-tip pen, a carpenter's square, and a long straightedge.

Using a linoleum or utility knife or heavy-duty scissors, cut the flooring roughly 3 inches over-size on all sides. The excess will be trimmed away after the flooring has been positioned.

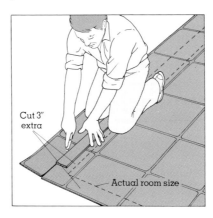

Cut 3" extra

Actual room size

If adhesive is required with your flooring, it can either be spread over the entire subfloor or, depending on the type of adhesive, spread in steps as the flooring is unrolled. Check the adhesive's "open-time"—the time it takes to dry.

Remove the baseboards and moldings from walls and cabinet fronts. Carry the roll of flooring into the kitchen and lay the longest edge against the longest wall, allowing the 3-inch excess to curl up the wall. The flooring should also curl up each adjoining wall. If the entire floor has been covered with adhesive, slowly roll the flooring out across the room. Take care to set the flooring firmly into the adhesive as you proceed. When you finish, start at the center of the room and work out any air bubbles that may remain. You can use a rolling pin for this, or rent a floor roller.

Installing flooring with seams. Transfer your floor plan or paper pattern to the flooring as described above. On flooring with a decorative pattern, be sure to leave the margins necessary to match the pattern at the seam on adjoining sheets (see below). If your flooring has a simulated grout or mortar joint, plan to cut the seam along the midpoint of the printed joint.

Cut the piece that requires the most intricate fitting first. If using adhesive, spread it on the subfloor as directed, stopping 8 or 9 inches from the seam. Then position the sheet on the floor. If you're not using adhesive, simply put the first sheet in place.

Next cut the second sheet of flooring and position it to overlap the first sheet by at least 2 inches; make sure the design is perfectly aligned. Again, if using adhesive, stop 8 or 9 inches from the seam; if not, position, the second sheet carefully, then secure it to the subfloor with two or three strips of double-faced tape.

When the flooring is in position, trim away excess material at each end of the seam in a half-moon shape so the ends butt against the wall (see drawing above right).

HOW TO MAKE SEAMS

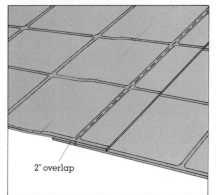

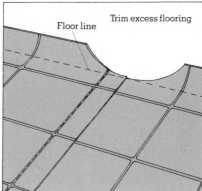

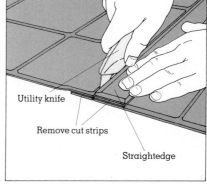

Overlap sheets at least 2 inches; be certain the design is perfectly aligned.

Trim excess flooring in a half-moon shape so the ends butt against the wall.

Cut down through both sheets along a straightedge, then remove the cut strips.

Using a steel straightedge and a sharp utility knife, make a straight cut—about ½ to ⅝ inch from the edge of the top sheet—down through both sheets of flooring. Lift up the flooring and spread adhesive under the seam—or if you're not using adhesive, apply a long piece of double-faced tape beneath the seam. Clean the area around the seam, using the appropriate solvent for your adhesive. Fuse the two pieces with a recommended seam sealer.

Trimming to fit. You'll need to make a series of relief cuts at all inside and outside corners to allow the flooring to lie flat on the floor.

At inside corners, gradually trim away the excess with diagonal cuts until the flooring lies flat (see drawing below). At outside corners, start

at the top of the lapped-up flooring and cut straight down to the point where the wall and floor meet.

After you cut the corners, remove the material lapped up against the walls. Using an 18 to 24-inch-long piece of 2 by 4, press the flooring into a right angle where the floor and wall join.

Lay a heavy metal straightedge along the wall and trim the flooring with a utility knife, leaving a gap of about ⅛ inch between the edge of the flooring and the wall. This will allow the material to expand without buckling; the baseboard and/or shoe molding will cover the gap. If you're planning to attach vinyl wall base (see below), be sure the base will overlap the edge of the flooring at least ¼ inch.

The most effective way to hide

an exposed edge around a doorway is to cut away just enough of the door casing to permit the flooring to slide underneath.

Finishing touches. When the new flooring has been cleaned and is flat and well-settled, replace any baseboards that have been removed. Then reattach the shoe molding, leaving a ¹⁄₃₂ to ¹⁄₁₆-inch gap between the flooring and the bottom of the molding. Always drive nails through the molding into the baseboards, never down into the flooring.

Vinyl wall base, an alternative to baseboards and molding, is fastened directly to the wall or base cabinets with adhesive; the lower edge rests on, but is not attached to, the flooring. Finally, finish your new floor as recommended.

(Continued on next page)

HOW TO TRIM FLOORING

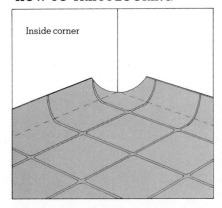

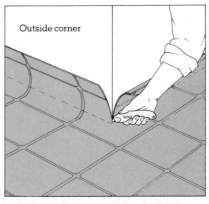

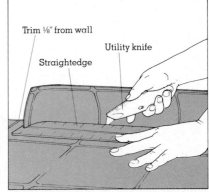

Where flooring turns an inside corner, cut the excess with diagonal cuts.

At outside corner, cut straight down to the point where wall and floor meet.

Trim flooring, leaving a ⅛" gap between the edge and the wall.

... Flooring

Ceramic tile floors

You can install a ceramic tile floor in a three-step operation: lay evenly spaced tiles in a bed of adhesive atop a smooth, dry, and rigid subfloor; fill the joint spaces between tiles with grout; and seal the floor for durability and easy cleaning. Glazed tiles, Type I mastic adhesive, and cement-based grout are probably the best materials for the kitchen do-it-yourselfer.

Preparing the subfloor. If at all possible, remove old flooring before installing new ceramic tiles. Not only does this enable you to examine the subfloor and make any necessary repairs, but it should also make the new floor level with floors in adjacent rooms. But if your old resilient (solid, not cushioned), ceramic tile, wood, or masonry flooring is level and in good repair, it can be successfully covered with tile. Your tile dealer can recommend the best adhesive and method of application.

To prepare a plywood subfloor, make certain that all panels are securely attached to the joists. If the subfloor is constructed from individual 4 or 6-inch boards, be sure that each board is securely attached. Drive any protruding nails flush with the surface.

To prevent a board subfloor from warping, or if the plywood subfloor is in poor condition, you'll have to install a new layer over the old before laying tile. Use exterior or underlayment-grade plywood or particle board at least ⅜ inch thick, and leave a 1/16-inch gap between adjacent panels. Fasten the panels with 6-penny ring-shank nails spaced 6 inches apart. Where possible, drive nails through the panels into the floor joists.

Regardless of your subfloor material, you may need to use a sealer before applying adhesive. Check your adhesive for instructions.

Establish working lines. The key to laying straight rows of tile is to establish proper working lines. You can begin either at the center of the room or at one wall.

If two adjoining walls meet at an exact right angle, start laying tiles along one wall. This method means that fewer border tiles need to be cut; it also allows you to work without stepping on rows previously set.

To check for square corners and straight walls, place a tile tightly into each corner. Stretch a chalkline between the corners of each pair of tiles; pull the line tight and snap each line. Variations in the distance between chalklines and walls will reveal any irregularities in the walls. You can ignore variations as slight as the width of a grout joint. With a carpenter's square, check the intersection of lines in each corner of the room.

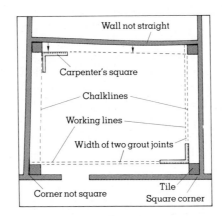

Assuming that your walls are reasonably straight, you can begin laying tile at any straight wall adjoining a straight corner. Snap a new chalkline parallel to the original line and approximately two grout joint widths closer to the center of the room (see drawing above). Lay a similar line, at a right angle to the first, along the adjoining wall. Then nail a batten (wood straightedge) along each of these working lines.

If you can't find a square corner, begin at the center of the room. Locate the center point on each of two opposite walls, and snap a chalkline between the two points. Then find the centers of the other two walls and stretch your chalkline at right angles to the first line; snap the line only after you've used your carpenter's square to determine that the two lines cross at a precise right angle.

Whether you begin at a wall or in the center, it's a good idea to make a dry run before you actually set the tiles in adhesive. Lay the tiles out on the lines, allowing proper spacing for grout joints. Try to determine the best layout while keeping the number of tiles to be cut to a minimum.

Setting the tiles. Using a notched trowel, start spreading a strip of adhesive along one of the battens. Cover about a square yard at first, or the area you can comfortably tile before the adhesive begins to set.

Using a gentle twisting motion, place the first tile in the corner formed by the two battens. With the same motion, place a second tile alongside the first. To establish the proper width for the grout joint, use molded plastic spacers. Continue laying tiles along the batten until the row is complete. Start each new row at the same end as the first. If you're working from the center of the room, follow one of the patterns shown below.

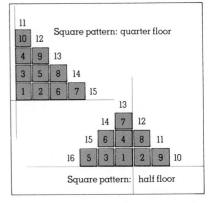

As the tiles are laid, set a piece of carpet-wrapped wood over the tiles; tap it with a mallet or hammer to "beat in" the tiles. Keep checking with a carpenter's square or straightedge to make sure each course is straight. Wiggle any stray tiles back into position while the adhesive is still flexible.

When you're ready to install border tiles, carefully remove the battens. Measure the remaining spaces individually, subtract the width of two grout joints, and mark each tile for any necessary cuts.

HOW TO SET CERAMIC FLOOR TILES

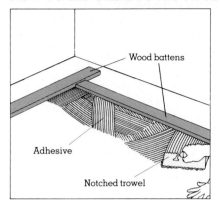

Nail batten boards at right angles, flush with the working lines. Then spread adhesive alongside one batten with a notched trowel.

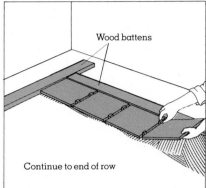

Begin placing tiles from the corner formed by the battens, using spacers to maintain the width of the grout joint. Continue to the end of the first row.

Start each new row at the same end as the first row. To set tiles in adhesive, slide a beating block (padded wood block) over the tiles while tapping it with a hammer.

You can cut tile with a tile cutter rented from your tile supplier; or you can (A) score tile with a glass cutter and straightedge, then (B) press it down evenly over a ¼-inch dowel (see below). To cut irregular shapes, use a tile nipper; first score the cutting lines with a glass cutter.

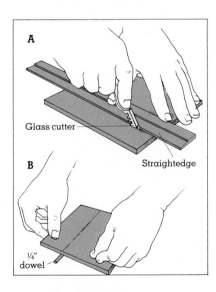

After all the tiles are placed, remove any spacers and clean the tile surface so it's completely free of adhesive. Before applying grout, allow the tiles to set properly—about 24 hours with mastic adhesives.

Applying grout. Grout can be applied liberally around glazed tiles. Grouting unglazed tiles requires more care, since the grout may stain the tile's surface. Be sure to read the manufacturer's recommendations.

Using a rubber-faced float or squeegee, apply grout to the surface of the tile. Force the grout into the joints so they're completely filled; make sure no air pockets remain. Scrape off excess grout with the float, working diagonally across the tiles.

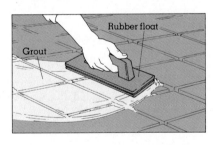

Soak a sponge in clear water and wring it out. Wipe the tiles with a circular motion, removing any remaining grout, until the joints are smooth and level with the tiles. Rinse and wring out the sponge frequently.

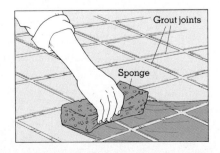

When the tiles are clean, let the grout dry for about 30 minutes. By then, any film of grout left on the tile will have formed a light haze; immediately polish it off with a soft cloth. Smooth the grout joints with a jointer, striking tool, or toothbrush.

Finishing touches. Most grouts take at least 2 weeks to cure. You'll need to damp-cure a cement-based grout by covering the newly installed floor with plastic. Leave the plastic in place for 24 hours; then remove it and allow the grout to cure thoroughly. Stay off the tile until cured.

Once the grout has fully cured, seal it and the tile with a silicone or lacquer-base sealer recommended by your tile supplier.

Wood strip flooring

Wood strip flooring, the most popular "hardwood" floor, is made up of narrow boards with tongue-and-groove edges and ends, laid in random lengths.

You can buy finished or unfinished wood strips. The latter is the best choice for kitchen flooring—the ability to seal joints between the strips is a must for water-resistance.

Though widths and thicknesses vary, the most common strip flooring for finishing in place is ¾ inch or ²⁵⁄₃₂ inch thick, with a face width of 2¼ inches.

(Continued on next page)

... Flooring

Preparing the subfloor. The subfloor preparation can be more demanding than putting in the new flooring. Moisture is the number one enemy of wood floors; you must ensure that the subfloor is completely dry and will remain dry. Any crawlspace below the floor must also be properly ventilated and protected from moisture.

Though it's possible to lay wood flooring over an old wood floor that's structurally sound and perfectly level, you may need to remove the old flooring to get down to the subfloor and make necessary repairs or install underlayment. In the long run, this usually provides the most reliable base for your new floor.

Check the exposed subfloor for loose boards or loose plywood panels. If planks are badly bowed and cannot be flattened by nailing, give the floor a rough sanding with a floor sander (see page 133) or cover it with ⅜ or ½-inch plywood or particle board. Fasten down ⅜-inch material with 3-penny ring-shank or cement-coated nails; for ½-inch material, use 4-penny ring-shank or 5-penny cement-coated nails. Space nails 6 inches apart across the surface of the panels.

New or old, the base for the new floor should be cleaned thoroughly, then covered with a layer of 15-pound asphalt-saturated felt (butting seams) or soft resin paper (overlapping seams 4 inches).

As you put the felt or paper in place, use a straightedge or a chalkline to mark the center of each joist on the covering. The lines will serve as reference points when you attach the new flooring.

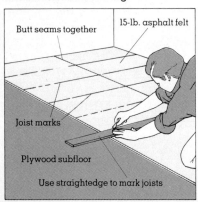

Butt seams together · 15-lb. asphalt felt · Joist marks · Plywood subfloor · Use straightedge to mark joists

Planning the new floor. For a trouble-free installation, the first course you lay must be parallel to the center of the kitchen.

Measure the width of the room in several spots and locate the center line as accurately as possible. Snap a chalkline to mark the center, your primary reference point.

Next, measuring from the center line, lay out and snap another chalkline about ½ inch from the wall you're using as a starting point.

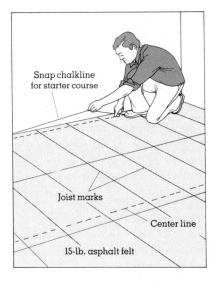

Snap chalkline for starter course · Joist marks · Center line · 15-lb. asphalt felt

In a kitchen that's obviously irregular in shape, locate the center line as closely as possible and begin laying the first row of flooring from that point. A special wood strip called a *spline* is used to join two back-to-back grooved boards along the center line.

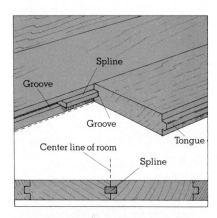

Spline · Groove · Groove · Center line of room · Tongue · Spline

Installing the flooring. When starting from the wall, you may need to trim a few boards at the outset. It's important that your first row of flooring line up properly while keeping the ½-inch distance from the wall. If you're starting from the center of an irregular room, the trimming will be done later when you reach the walls.

Tongue-and-groove strip flooring is attached by nailing at an angle through the tongues, where nail heads won't show. (This is called "blind-nailing.") To ensure a tight floor, install strips perpendicular to joists.

You can make a perfectly acceptable installation using basic hand tools, but a nailer—available from most tool rental companies—will speed up the work. Similarly, boards can be neatly cut with a back saw and miter box, but a radial-arm or table saw saves time and labor.

If you're starting along the wall, the first row of boards should be secured by face-nailing; the nails will be covered later with shoe molding. Predrill the boards with holes slightly smaller than the diameter of your nails.

When beginning at the center of an irregularly shaped room, you can start right off by blind-nailing through the tongues—with the nailer, if you have one.

Lay out boards six or seven rows ahead. This will help you plan an effective and attractive pattern. Stagger end joints so that no joint is closer than 6 inches to a joint in an adjoining row of boards. Leave approximately ½ inch between each end piece and the wall. As a general rule, no end piece should be shorter than 8 inches. When laying flooring over plywood or particle board, avoid placing the end joints in the flooring directly over joints in the subfloor.

As you place each row, move a block of wood along the leading edge of the flooring you've just put down, and give it a sharp rap with a mallet or hammer before you drive each nail. To avoid damaging the tongues, cut a groove in the block to accommodate the tongue, or use a short length of flooring.

Since you won't have enough space to use a nailer until you are several rows from the wall, you'll

HOW TO LAY WOOD STRIP FLOORING

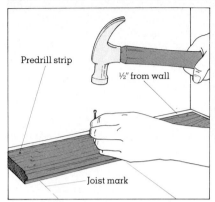

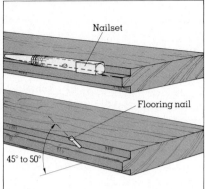

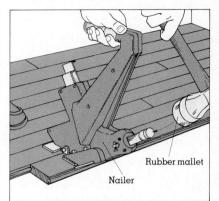

Predrill holes slightly smaller than the nail diameter, then face-nail the first course from the wall.

Nail first few rows by hand—start with a hammer, then drive the nail home with a nailset laid sideways along the tongue.

Once there's working room, drive nails with a nailer and rubber mallet; the nailer automatically drives nails flush.

have to nail the first courses by hand. By continuing to predrill holes for the nails, you can keep nails at the proper angle—45° to 50° from the floor—and help prevent splitting. Take care not to crush the upper edges of the boards. Instead of using your hammer to drive nails flush, leave the heads exposed; then place a nailset sideways over each nail along the top of the tongue, and tap the nailset with your hammer. Use the nailset's tip to drive the nail flush.

Once you have laid and nailed the first few rows by hand, you can begin to secure the flooring with a nailer, which automatically countersinks all the nails it drives.

When you reach the last few rows, you'll find it difficult to blind-nail the boards. Predrill holes and face-nail them. The final strip of flooring must be placed to leave a ½-inch gap between the flooring and the wall. If you're lucky, a standard board will fit. If not, you'll have to rip several boards down to the proper width.

If your new floor creates a change of level from one room to the next, smooth the transition with a rounded reducer strip.

Finishing touches. An unfinished floor will have to be sanded and finished. Most equipment rental companies offer the necessary heavy-duty equipment. The workhorse of this job is the floor (drum)

sander; look for a machine with a tilt-up lever that makes it possible to raise the drum off the floor without lifting the machine.

You'll also need an edging machine, a type of disk sander necessary for areas (next to a wall, for example) that can't be reached with a drum sander. A hand block and sandpaper are useful for corners and other tight spots.

When sanding a floor, you may also need a hammer and nailset to drive down protruding nail heads, and wood putty to fill holes, dents, and gouges.

Typically, three sandings—called "cuts"—using three grades of sandpaper are needed to prepare a floor for finishing. Floor sanding equipment, especially the unwieldy drum sander, must be operated with great care to avoid irrep-

arable damage to the new floor. For sanding techniques and procedures, see the Sunset book *Do-It-Yourself Flooring*, or ask your flooring supplier for recommendations.

Polyurethane has become today's dominant wood floor finish. It provides a hard, plasticlike surface that's impermeable to water and easy to care for.

To apply polyurethane, start with a clean brush along the walls and around obstacles. Then use a long-handled paint roller with a mohair cover to apply the finish evenly over the rest of the floor.

At least two (and preferably three) coats of polyurethane are the rule in the kitchen. Between coats, use a floor buffer equipped with #2 steel wool to smooth the surface. Corners and other hard-to-reach spots should be smoothed by hand.

FLOOR FINISHING TOOLS

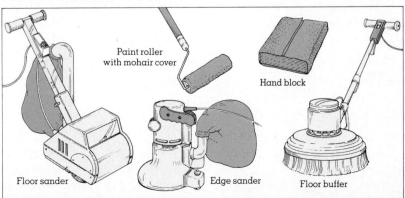

Fixtures & appliances

The various array of styles, colors and features available in kitchen fixtures and appliances can be bewildering. Disk faucets, double self-rimmed sinks, built-in dishwashers and microwave ovens are a few of the many choices you must make when remodeling a kitchen.

Fortunately for the do-it-yourselfer, most variations of the basic fixtures and appliances are installed in a similar manner. The following pages cover the fundamentals. Specific instructions should accompany each unit (check before purchase); follow the manufacturer's instructions if they differ from those below.

Many fixtures and appliances can be easily connected to an existing sink drain or electrical outlet. But before you make any purchase, be sure your home's plumbing and electrical systems can handle the new load. For a discussion of plumbing and electrical systems, their limitations, and applicable codes, see "Plumbing basics," pages 104–106, and "Electrical basics" pages 107–111.

Sometimes the greatest challenge of replacing a major appliance such as a refrigerator, is transporting the old one from the site and bringing in the new one. Always plan your route in advance ("Do we need to remove a door? How will we get it down the steps?"), and have adequate help on hand. An appliance dolly can be indispensable.

Installing a faucet

Most modern kitchen faucets are the deck-mounted type, seated on the rear of the sink and secured from below. When shopping for a replacement, you'll find the selection staggering. You can choose from a lineup of single-handled washerless faucets—valve, disk, ball, and cartridge—and styles ranging from antique reproductions to futuristic compression models. All are interchangeable as long as the new faucet's inlet shanks are spaced to fit the holes on the sink.

If you still have old-fashioned wall-mounted faucets, you face a different decision: either buy an updated style, or switch to a deck-mounted type. Switching types adds several steps to the installation process; at the minimum, you'll need to reroute pipes from the wall into the kitchen cabinet and patch the wall. For help with either choice, see the *Sunset* book *Basic Plumbing Illustrated*.

Removing a deck-mounted faucet. Begin by shutting off the water supply, either at the shutoff valves on both hot and cold water supply lines or (if you don't have shutoff valves) at the main house shutoff near the water meter. Then drain the pipes by opening the faucet or faucets.

Use a wrench to unfasten the couplings that attach the supply tubing to the shutoff valves. Since space is cramped under the sink, use a basin wrench to loosen and remove the locknuts and washers on both faucet inlet shanks.

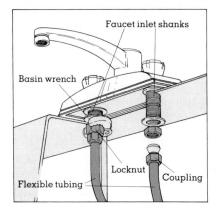

On a kitchen sink with a spray hose attachment, use the basin wrench to undo the locknuts connecting the hose to the faucet body and the hose nipple. Then lift the faucet away from the sink.

Installing the new faucet. Clean the surface of the sink where the new faucet will sit. Most faucets come with a rubber gasket on the bottom; if yours doesn't, apply plumber's putty to the base.

Set the faucet in position, simultaneously feeding the flexible supply tubing, if attached, down through the middle sink hole. (If your new faucet has no tubing included, buy two lengths of tubing and attach them at this point.) Press the

HOW TO INSTALL FAUCETS

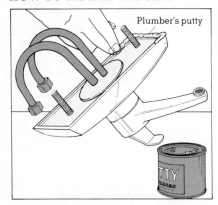

Apply plumber's putty to the bottom edge of the faucet body if there's no gasket to seal it to the sink's surface.

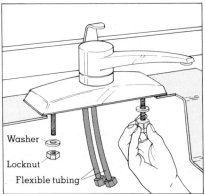

Set the faucet in place, threading supply tubes through the sink hole; then tighten the locknuts.

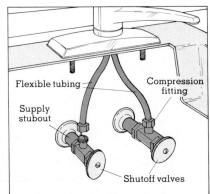

Attach flexible tubing to the shutoff valves, using appropriate compression fittings.

faucet onto the sink's surface. Place the washers and locknuts on the faucet inlet shanks; tighten them with a basin wrench. Attach a spray hose according to the manufacturer's instructions.

Run the flexible tubing to the shutoff valves, gently bending the tubing as necessary, and connect it using compression fittings. (If you'd like to install shutoff valves in your system, see the *Sunset* book *Basic Plumbing Illustrated.)*

Installing a sink

A deck-mounted kitchen sink fits into a specially cut hole in the countertop. If you're simply replacing a sink, you can choose any model the same size as the present sink, or *larger;* if it's a new installation, you'll have to make the sink cutout first.

Three basic sink types prevail: frame-rimmed, self-rimmed, and

SINK DRAIN ELEMENTS

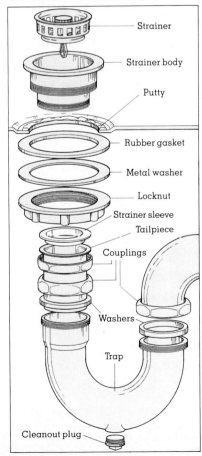

- Strainer
- Strainer body
- Putty
- Rubber gasket
- Metal washer
- Locknut
- Strainer sleeve
- Tailpiece
- Couplings
- Washers
- Trap
- Cleanout plug

unrimmed. A frame-rimmed sink has a surrounding metal channel that holds the sink to the countertop; a self-rimmed sink has a molded overlap that's supported by the countertop cutout; and an unrimmed sink is recessed beneath the countertop cutout and held in place by metal clips.

Removing an old sink. First shut off the water supply at the shutoff valves on both hot and cold water supply pipes; if you don't have shutoff valves, turn off the water at the main house shutoff. Then drain the pipes by opening both faucets, and disconnect the supply pipes as described on page 134. You'll also need to disconnect the drain trap from the sink's strainer assembly. Loosen the couplings that hold the tailpiece to the strainer assembly, and the tailpiece to the trap. Push the tailpiece down into the trap.

From below the sink, remove any clamps or lugs holding it to the countertop. If necessary, break the putty seal by forcing the sink free.

Making a sink cutout. For a new installation, trace either a template (included with the new sink) or the bottom edge of the frame onto the exact spot where the sink will sit. Typically, 1½ to 2 inches is left between the edge of the cutout and the front edge of the countertop. Drill pilot holes in each corner of the outline, and insert a saber saw into one of the holes to make the cutout.

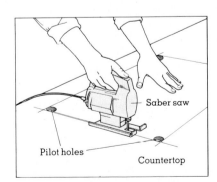

Saber saw
Pilot holes
Countertop

Installing the new sink. It's best to mount the faucet and hook up the strainer assembly before installing the new sink in the countertop.

To install a strainer assembly, first apply a bead of plumber's putty to the underlip of the strainer body, then press it down into the sink opening. If the strainer is held in place by a locknut, place the rubber gasket and metal washer over the strainer body, and tighten by hand. Hold the strainer from above while you snug up the locknut, preferably with a spud wrench. If the strainer is held in place by a retainer, fit the retainer over the strainer body and tighten all three screws. Attach the tailpiece with a coupling.

For a frame-rimmed sink, apply a ring of plumber's putty around the top edge of the sink. Fasten the frame to the sink, following the manufacturer's instructions; some frames attach with metal corner clamps, others with metal extension tabs that bend around the sink lip. Wipe off excess putty.

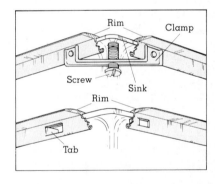

Rim
Clamp
Screw
Sink
Rim
Tab

Before installing a deck-mounted sink of any style, apply a ½-inch-wide strip of putty or silicone sealant along the edge of the countertop opening. Set the sink into the cutout, pressing it down. Smooth excess putty.

Anchor the sink from below at 6 or 8-inch intervals, using any clamps or lugs provided. Hook up the supply pipes and drain trap.

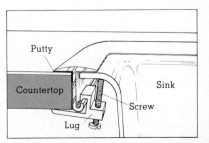

Putty
Countertop
Sink
Screw
Lug

(Continued on next page)

... Fixtures & appliances

Installing a garbage disposer

Installing a disposer takes a few hours, but the basic connection is not difficult. Most units fit the standard 3½ or 4-inch drain outlets of kitchen sinks and mount somewhat like a sink strainer (see page 135).

Plumbing a disposer involves altering the sink trap to fit the unit. If your model has direct wiring, you must run electrical cable to a nearby junction box or other power source (see pages 107–111 for information). Plug-in disposers require a 120-volt grounded (three-prong) outlet under the sink, and a separate wall switch adjacent to the sink.

Before installing a disposer, check plumbing codes for any restrictions.

Removing a strainer or disposer. If you're adding a disposer for the first time, first disconnect the sink strainer assembly. Start by removing the tailpiece and trap (see page 135); then disassemble the strainer components and lift them out of the sink. Clean away any old putty or sealing gaskets around the opening.

If you're replacing a disposer, first turn off the electricity (see page 107); then unplug the unit or disconnect the wiring. Loosen the screws on the mounting ring assembly and remove the parts; finally, remove the sink flange from above.

Mounting the disposer. The disposer comes with its own sink flange and mounting assembly. Run a bead of plumber's putty around the sink opening and seat the flange. Then, working from below, slip the gasket, mounting rings, and snap ring up onto the neck of the flange. The snap ring should fit firmly into a groove on the sink flange to hold things in place temporarily.

Uniformly tighten the slotted screws in the mounting rings until the gasket fits snugly against the bottom of the flange. Remove any excess putty from around the flange.

Attach the drain elbow to the disposer. Lift the disposer into place, aligning the holes in the disposer's flange with the slotted screws in the mounting rings. Rotate the disposer so that the drain elbow lines up with the drainpipe. Tighten the nuts securely onto the slotted screws to ensure a good seal.

Making the hookups. Fit the coupling and washer onto the drain elbow. Add an elbow fitting on the other end of the trap to adjust to the drainpipe. You may need to shorten the drainpipe to make the connection. Tighten all connections, and

run water down through the disposer to check for leaks.

At this point, either plug the disposer into a grounded outlet (see pages 110–111) or shut off the power and wire the unit directly, following the manufacturer's instructions. Then turn the power back on. To be safe, test the unit for proper grounding (for techniques, see the *Sunset* book *Basic Home Wiring Illustrated*).

Installing a dishwasher

A built-in dishwasher requires three connections; hot water supply, drainpipe fitting, and a 120-volt, 20-amp, grounded plug-in outlet. (For basic electrical information, see pages 107–111.)

Local codes may require that you also install a venting device, called an air gap, on the sink or countertop. Some municipalities require a permit and an inspection when a built-in dishwasher is installed; check before you begin the work.

Making new connections. For a first-time installation, you'll need to tap into the hot water supply pipe under the sink, and into either the garbage disposer or sink drainpipe for proper drainage.

HOW TO PLUMB A GARBAGE DISPOSER

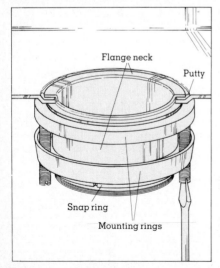

Attach mounting rings, with gasket and snap ring, to the sink flange; tighten the slotted screws.

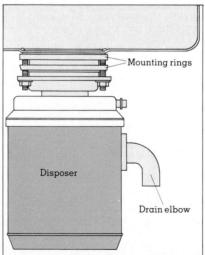

Line up the drain elbow on the disposer so it's directly opposite the drainpipe; tighten nuts onto the slotted screws.

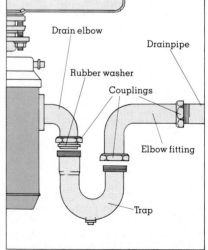

Connect the trap to the disposer's drain elbow and to the elbow fitting on the drainpipe.

Begin by shutting off the water supply, either at the shutoff valves under the sink or at the main house shutoff. Drain the supply pipes by turning on the sink faucets. Cut into the hot water supply pipe and install a tee fitting. (If you need a course in pipefitting techniques, see the *Sunset* book *Basic Plumbing Illustrated*.) Run flexible copper or plastic tubing to the location of the water inlet valve on the dishwasher. To simplify future repairs, install a shutoff valve along the tubing.

Your dishwasher can drain either into the sink drain above the trap or into a garbage disposer. For use with a sink drain, you'll need to buy a threaded waste tee fitting (see drawing below).

To install a waste tee, remove the sink tailpiece *(see page 135)* and insert the waste tee into the trap. Cut the tailpiece so it fits between the waste tee and the sink strainer assembly. Reattach the tailpiece, and clamp the dishwasher drain hose onto the waste tee fitting.

If you already have (or are installing) a garbage disposer, plan to attach the dishwasher drain hose to the disposer drain fitting on the disposer's side. First turn off the electrical circuit that controls the disposer. Then use a screwdriver to punch out the knockout plug inside the fitting. Clamp the dishwasher drain hose to the fitting.

To prevent a backup of waste water into the dishwasher, make a gradual loop with the drain hose to the height of the dishwasher's top before making the connection. If you're required to install an air gap instead of the loop, insert the air gap into the predrilled hole found on some sinks, or into a hole you've drilled at the back of the countertop. Screw the air gap tight from below.

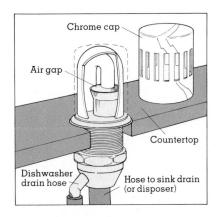

Run one length of hose from the dishwasher to the air gap, and another from the air gap to the waste tee or disposer.

Removing an old dishwasher. If you're simply replacing a dishwasher, the connections should already be made. But you'll have to disconnect and remove the old unit before installing the new one.

First, unfasten any screws or brackets anchoring the unit to the countertop or the floor. Turn off electrical power to the circuit controlling the dishwasher; then shut off the water supply. Disconnect the supply hookup and the drain hose from the dishwasher. With a helper, pull the unit forward to gain access to the electrical connection (unless it's simply under the sink). If the dishwasher is the plug-in type, you're in luck. If it was wired directly, disconnect the wires from the dishwasher.

Completing the installation. Plug in the new dishwasher, then slide it into place. To add a new plug-in outlet, see pages 110–111, or consult a professional electrician. Complete the supply and drain hookups according to the manufacturer's instructions.

Once it's hooked up, level the dishwasher by adjusting the height of the legs. Anchor the unit to the underside of the countertop with any screws provided.

(Continued on next page)

HOW TO CONNECT A DISHWASHER

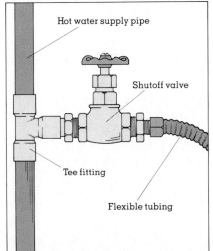

Install a tee fitting and shutoff valve in the hot water supply pipe, then run flexible tubing to the dishwasher.

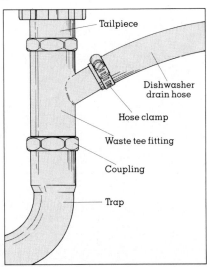

To drain into a sink trap, add a threaded waste tee fitting between tailpiece and trap.

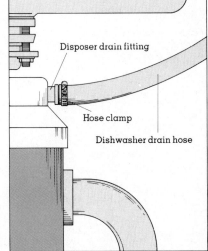

To drain into a garbage disposer, connect a dishwasher drain hose to the disposer's drain fitting.

... Fixtures & appliances

Installing a hot water dispenser

Easy-to-install hot water dispensers incorporate a stainless steel faucet connected to an under-counter storage tank. The tank, which in turn is connected to a nearby cold water pipe, has an electric heating coil that keeps water at about 200°F—50° hotter than that produced by the average water heater.

Most units plug into a 120-volt grounded outlet installed under the sink. *(For electrical details, see pages 107–111.)* Some models, though, are directly wired to a grounded junction box.

Positioning the dispenser. Begin by deciding where you want to place the unit. Commonly, the faucet fits in a hole at the rear of the sink rim, or else mounts directly on the countertop. In the latter case, cut a 1¼-inch-diameter hole in your counter-top near the sink rim with a hole saw or electric drill. Following the manufacturer's instructions, attach the dispenser faucet from beneath the sink. Generally, you'll need only to install a nut and washers to hold the faucet.

From inside the sink cabinet, screw the tank mounting bracket to the wall or cabinet back, making sure it's plumb. The bracket should be located about 14 inches below the underside of the countertop. Next, mount the tank on the bracket.

Making the connections. Before plumbing the unit, shut off the water supply and drain the pipes by opening the sink faucets. Many dispensers come with a self-tapping valve. If yours doesn't, tap into the cold water pipe using a saddle tee fitting (see drawing below). To do this, clamp the fitting to the supply pipe and drill a hole through the fitting into the pipe.

If saddle tees aren't permitted in your area, tap in with a standard tee fitting, then install a shutoff valve and reducer fitting for the dispenser's water supply tube. (For pipefitting techniques, see the *Sunset* book *Basic Plumbing Illustrated.*)

Using the compression nuts provided with the unit, attach one incoming water supply tube between the dispenser and the storage tank, and another between the tank and the cold water supply pipe. Turn on the water supply and check for leaks. Plug in the unit—or shut off the power and connect the wires directly, as required. Finally, turn the power on.

Installing a refrigerator

Installing a new refrigerator is easy work—just plug it in to a 120-volt, 20-amp appliance circuit. Your only real challenge will be handling and transporting both the old and the new units.

Disconnecting a refrigerator. When removing the old refrigerator, simply pull it out any way you can to gain access to the plug. If the unit has an automatic icemaker, the fitting attaching the copper supply tubing must be disconnected. Be prepared to remove doors from their hinges, guard rails from stairways, or any other obstructions in the path. Then secure the refrigerator to an appliance dolly and wheel it out.

Positioning a new refrigerator. Wheel the replacement into a position where you can hook up the ice-maker, if necessary, and plug the refrigerator in. Finally push it into place and check level. Adjust the level with shims, as necessary.

A refrigerator can be given a "built-in" look—just wrap modular cabinets around it, or install custom-made cabinets. Be sure to allow ½ inch to 1 inch around all sides for easy removal and air circulation. For a different built-in look, face the refrigerator on one side with an end panel to match the cabinetry; panels are available with most modular cabinet lines.

HOW TO HOOK UP A HOT WATER DISPENSER

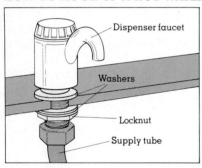

First, secure the dispenser faucet to the sink rim or countertop from below, using nut and washers.

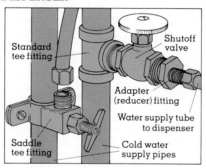

Tap into the cold water supply pipe with a saddle tee or standard tee fitting and shutoff valve.

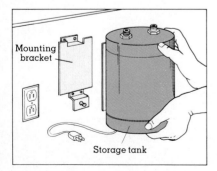

Attach the tank mounting bracket to the wall or cabinet back, then install the storage tank.

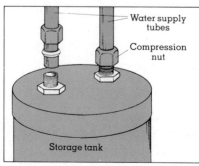

Hook up one supply tube from the dispenser to the storage tank, and one from the tank to the supply pipe.

Installing an icemaker. An automatic icemaker is connected by ¼-inch copper tubing to a cold water supply pipe. To make the connection, use a saddle tee or standard tee fitting and shutoff valve, as detailed under "Installing a hot water dispenser," at left. If the refrigerator can be easily reached from the sink complex, tap in there and drill small access holes through the sides of the base cabinets to route the tubing. If the refrigerator is far from the sink, look for another cold water supply pipe to tap *(see pages 104–106 for help).*

At the refrigerator end, leave a few extra loops of tubing to help you position the unit. Attach the tubing to the refrigerator with a compression union (see drawing below) or other special fitting, following the manufacturer's instructions.

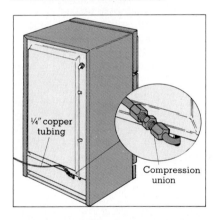

¼" copper tubing

Compression union

Installing a trash compactor

A new trash compactor, like a refrigerator, is simple to hook up—just plug it into a 120-volt, 20-amp grounded outlet. Again, like the refrigerator, your major task is moving it into position.

A typical compactor fits into the same space as a standard 15-inch-wide base cabinet; it can be built in under the countertop, enclosed with an end panel, or used as a free-standing unit.

To install the compactor, move it roughly into position until you can plug in the power cord. Then wrestle it into place (taking care not to scratch the flooring) and level the unit, either by shimming or by adjusting any built-in legs.

Installing cooktops, ranges & wall ovens

Cooking equipment offers you a choice of two energy sources—electricity or gas. In addition it offers three basic designs to choose from— a free-standing or "slide-in" range, a drop-in range, or a combination of built-in cooktop and separate wall ovens.

The only factors limiting your choice are the capacity of your present gas or electrical system, the distance from an existing connection that you plan to move new equipment, and the labor and expense of switching from electricity to gas, or vice versa.

To analyze your present electrical system, see pages 107–108. An electric range, or wall ovens and a separate cooktop, must be powered by an individual 120/240-volt, 50-amp circuit. (The exception is a microwave oven, which requires only 120-volt current.) The power cords on the appliances must be equipped with special 50-amp plugs and attached to special 50-amp outlets. If you need to add a new circuit, see the *Sunset* book *Basic Home Wiring Illustrated,* or consult a licensed electrician.

For a discussion of gas system basics, see page 106. A gas range can usually be relocated as far as 6 feet from the old gas connection, if you plan to use the existing line. For new gas lines, you should hire a licensed plumber unless you're very well versed in gas installations. In any case, the work will require inspection by your building department before hookup.

Once your electrical or gas lines are in order, the actual hookup is straightforward.

Removing a range, oven, or cook-top. Before removing the old unit, first determine the method by which it is fastened (if it is fastened); for help, refer to the appropriate section on page 140. You'll probably need to unfasten some screws or clamps attaching the unit to the underside of the countertop, or to adjacent cabinets.

After removing the fasteners, move the appliance just far enough to gain access to the electrical or gas connection. If the appliance is electric, shut off the circuit to the appliance or appliance group before beginning the removal.

Gas appliances have individual shutoff valves (see drawing below). The valve is open when the handle is *parallel* to the pipe; to shut off the gas supply, turn the handle until it forms a *right angle* with the pipe. The appliance is connected to the shutoff valve and main gas line with either solid pipe or flexible tubing and compression fittings.

Solid pipe will need to be cut or unthreaded. A flexible connector can be removed from the shutoff valve with an adjustable wrench.

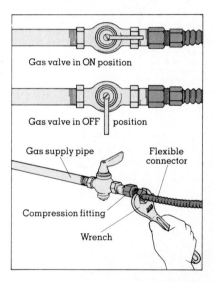

Gas valve in ON position

Gas valve in OFF position

Gas supply pipe

Flexible connector

Compression fitting

Wrench

Some gas appliances also have a 120-volt electrical connection that powers lights, timers, or thermostat. Unplug it or, if the connection is wired directly, shut off power to the circuit before disconnecting the wires.

If at any point you're unsure about how to proceed, call your utility company or seek other knowledgeable help.

Once both the fasteners and power connection are disassembled, the unit can be freely lifted or pulled out of position, loaded onto an appliance dolly, and transported from the room. Be sure you have adequate help for heavy jobs.

(Continued on next page)

... Fixtures & appliances

Installing a freestanding range. Except for the bulkiness of these units, this is a simple job to perform. Be sure the gas shutoff valve or electrical outlet is already in place. Slide the unit in part way until you can make the power hookup; then position it exactly. If the range has adjustable legs, raise or lower them to level the unit; otherwise, use shims as necessary.

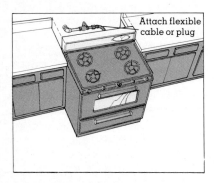

Attach flexible cable or plug

If you plan to use an existing gas connection, the new range must be within 6 feet of the shutoff valve. Check local gas or plumbing codes to determine if the connector may be flexible copper, brass, or aluminum, or if it must be solid pipe. A flexible connector is much simpler to install. Use an adjustable wrench to attach the connector's compression nuts to both range and shutoff as required.

Before turning the gas supply back on, it's wise to have utility company personnel check your work. They can inspect for gas leaks or air in the line, and can light and adjust the pilot lights on your new range.

Installing a drop-in range. This type of range is lowered into place between adjacent base cabinets. You'll need to determine the best method for attaching the power connection (either electric plug or gas connector) before, during, or after lifting the unit into place.

Some units have self-supporting flanges that sit on adjacent countertop surfaces. Others are simply lowered into place atop a special cabinet base. Fasten these ranges through side slots into the adjacent cabinets, or into the base itself. Bases and front trim that match

the surrounding cabinetry are available with many cabinet lines, or you can have them custom-made.

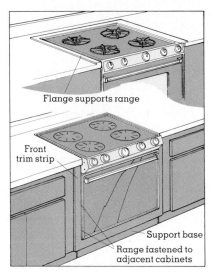

Flange supports range

Front trim strip

Support base

Range fastened to adjacent cabinets

Installing a cooktop. Standard electric and gas cooktops or combination cooktop-barbecue units are dropped into a countertop cutout, much as a new sink is installed (see page 135), then anchored from below with hardware supplied by the manufacturer. The power connection is in the cabinet directly below or to one side of the unit.

Electric cooktops may be plugged in or directly wired to a nearby junction box. A gas cooktop is normally connected by a flexible connector (check local codes), and must be located within 3 feet of its shutoff valve.

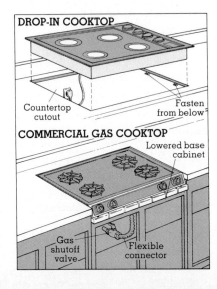

DROP-IN COOKTOP

Countertop cutout

Fasten from below

COMMERCIAL GAS COOKTOP

Lowered base cabinet

Gas shutoff valve

Flexible connector

Commercial gas cooktops sit on their own legs on the countertop. Often, a lowered base cabinet is used to align the cooktop with the surrounding countertop. Because of its resistance to heat, tile is frequently used below and surrounding the cooktop. The flexible gas connector is commonly run through a hole drilled in the countertop into the base cabinet below.

Many cooktops, especially those containing an indoor barbecue unit, have special downventing components that direct smoke, grease and moisture to a fan located in the base cabinet below. From that point, ducting runs out through the wall, or down through the cabinet base and below the floor.

Installing a wall oven. Separate wall ovens, either singly or in pairs, are housed in specially designed wall cabinets supplied in many sizes. Choose your wall oven first, and take the specifications with you when you shop for cabinets.

Wall ovens typically slide into place and rest atop support shelves. They're fastened to the cabinet through the sides or through overlapping flanges on the front. Trim strips are commonly available to fill any gaps between the ovens and the cabinet front.

The plug-in outlet or gas shutoff valve is usually located below the oven or ovens, inside the cabinet. If you plan both a microwave and a standard electric oven, you'll need both 120-volt and 120/240-volt outlets.

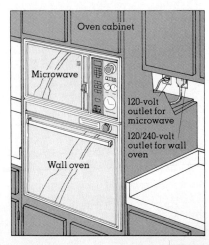

Oven cabinet

Microwave

120-volt outlet for microwave

120/240-volt outlet for wall oven

Wall oven

Installing a ventilation hood

The two basic types of ventilation hood are *ducted* and *ductless*. Though the ductless type is far easier to install (it requires no ductwork), the ducted version is far more efficient.

Before planning any ducting, or purchasing materials, check local mechanical codes for requirements.

Ducting basics. If you're simply replacing a ducted vent hood with a new one, you can probably use the old ducting to vent the new hood.

If you're starting from scratch, keep in mind that the straighter and shorter the path is from the hood to the outside, the more efficient the hood will be. Ducting can run either vertically through the roof or out through the wall, whichever is more direct and easier to install.

Ducting is available in both metal and plastic, and is either rectangular or round. The round type is available in both rigid and flexible varieties. The flexible type, though not as strong as the rigid sort, will follow a more twisted course without requiring fittings at each bend. However, if you use round ducting, you'll have to provide a transition fitting where the ducting meets the vent hood.

Join sections of ducting with duct tape. If any elbow fittings are re-

HOW TO MOUNT A VENT HOOD

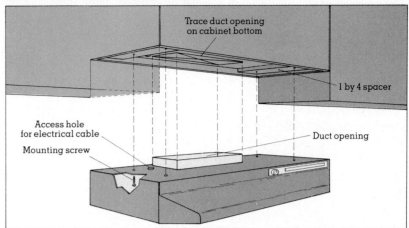

To mount a vent hood, trace the duct opening and electrical cable knockout hole on the wall cabinet or wall. Make the cutout with a drill and saber saw. If the cabinet bottom is recessed, add spacers to provide flush mounting surfaces.

quired, you'll need access to make the connection. Outside, protect the opening with either a flanged wall cap or a roof cap with integral flashing. Caulk around a wall cap to seal the seams between flange and siding. A roof cap's flashing must first be slipped under the roofing material; then all seams are liberally covered with roofing cement.

Mounting the hood. A vent hood is most commonly mounted on the bottom of an overhead wall cabinet. But first you must cut holes in the cabinet to correspond to knockout

holes on the vent's shell: one for the duct connector and one for the electrical cable.

Open the knockouts on the hood with a screwdriver and pliers. With a helper holding the hood flush with the front of the cabinet, trace the knockouts on the cabinet bottom. Drill out the electrical cable hole. Then drill pilot holes in the four corners of the duct connector outline, and cut out the area with a keyhole or saber saw.

The hood will mount to the bottom of the cabinet with screws provided; mark these spots next. If the cabinet's bottom is recessed, you'll have to add filler strips to attach the unit, as shown above. Then drill pilot holes for the screws. Adjusting the hood to fit perfectly flush with the cabinet front, fasten the hood to the cabinet. Thread the electrical cable through the appropriate cabinet hole, then through the knockout in the vent hood.

Hook up the electrical wires according to the manufacturer's instructions, making sure to attach the grounding screw to the grounding bracket on the hood.

Using duct tape or sheet metal screws, connect the vent hood's duct connector to the ducting inside the cabinet. Finally, install light bulbs, lighting panel, and filter panel.

TWO PATHS FOR A VENT DUCT

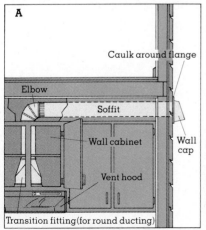

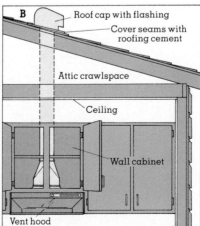

Two options for routing duct from a vent hood: run it horizontally in the space between wall cabinets and ceiling, or behind a soffit (A); or take the direct route up through the cabinet, ceiling, and attic to the roof (B).

INFORMATION SOURCES

When you're transforming an old kitchen into one that's innovative and workable, you'll find a wealth of ideas and information in brochures put out by the various manufacturers listed on these pages. They can also tell you about local outlets and distributors for their products. The addresses and phone numbers in this list are accurate as of press time.

The yellow pages of your telephone directory and the National Kitchen & Bath Association (124 Main Street, Hackettstown, NJ 07840) can help you locate kitchen showrooms, cabinetmakers, designers, architects, and other sources near you.

APPLIANCES

ABBAKA
435 23rd Street
San Francisco, CA 94107
415-648-7210

AEG
ANDI-CO. Appliances
65 Campus Plaza
Edison, NJ 08837
201-225-8837

AGA Cookers
Cooper & Turner, Inc.
R.F.D. 1, Box 477
Stowe, VT 05672
802-253-9729

Admiral Co.
Maycor Corp.
240 Edwards
Cleveland, TN 37311
615-472-3333

Amana Refrigeration, Inc.
Highway 220
Amana, IA 52204
319-622-5511

ASEA Dishwashers
ASKO Inc.
903 Bowser Street #170
Richardson, TX 75081
1-800-367-2444

Casablanca Fan Co.
PO Box 424
City of Industry, CA 91747
818-369-6441

Creda
1-800-99-CREDA

Dacor
950 S. Raymond Avenue
Pasadena, CA 91109
818-799-1000

Euroflair/Frigidaire
WCI Appliance Group
6000 Perimeter Drive
Dublin, OH 43017
1-800-451-7007

Gaggenau USA Corp.
425 University Avenue
Norwood, MA 02062
617-255-1766

GE/Hotpoint Appliances
General Electric Co.
Appliance Park
Louisville, KY 40225
800-626-2000

In-Sink-Erator
Emerson Electric Company
4700 21st Street
Racine, WI 53406
800-558-5712

Jenn-Air Co.
3035 N. Shadeland Avenue
Indianapolis, IN 46226
317-545-2271

KitchenAid, Inc.
701 Main Street
St. Joseph, MI 49085
616-982-4500

La Cornue Range
Purcell-Murray Co.
113 Park Lane
Brisbane, CA 94005
800-892-4040

Miele Appliances, Inc.
22D Worlds Fair Drive
Somerset, NJ 08873
201-560-0899

Modern Maid
403 N. Main Street
Topton, PA 19562
215-682-4211

NuTone, Inc.
Madison & Red Bank Roads
Cincinnati, OH 45227
513-527-5100

Sub-Zero Freezer Co.
PO Box 4130
Madison, WI 53711
608-271-2233

Thermador
5119 District Boulevard
Los Angeles, CA 90040
213-562-1133

Traulsen & Co., Inc.
114-02 15th Avenue
College Point, NY 11356
718-463-9000

Viking Range Corp.
PO Box 8012
Greenwood, MS 38930
601-455-1200

Whirlpool Corp.
2000 M63 North
Benton Harbor, MI 49022
800-253-1301

White-Westinghouse
4007 Paramount Boulevard,
Suite 100
Lakewood, CA 90712
800-421-2972
800-262-1969 (Calif)

Wolf Range Co.
19600 S. Alameda Street
PO Box 7050
Compton, CA 90224
213-774-7565

CABINETS

Allmilmö Corp.
70 Clinton Road
Fairfield, NJ 07004
201-227-2502

Dura Supreme
300 Dura Drive
Howard Lake, MN 55349
612-543-3872

Kraftmaid
16052 Industrial Parkway
Middlefield, OH 44062
216-632-5333

Merillat Industries, Inc.
5353 W, US 223
Adrian, MI 49221
517-263-0771

Poggenpohl USA Corp.
5905 Johns Road
Tampa, FL 33634
813-882-9292

Quaker Maid
WCI, Inc.
Route 61
Leesport, PA 19533
215-926-3011

Rutt Custom Kitchens
Route 23
Goodville, PA 17528
215-445-6751

Sears/Kenmore
Sears Tower
Department 703
Chicago, IL 60684
312-875-2500

SieMatic
One Neshaminy Interplex
Suite 207
Trevose, PA 19047
215-244-0700

**Smallbone Traditional
English Kitchens**
150 E. 58th Street
Suite 904
New York, NY 10155
212-935-3222

Snaidero West, Inc.
Pacific Design Center
8687 Melrose Avenue B487
Los Angeles, CA 90069
213-854-0222

Wm Ohs Cabinets
5095 Peoria Street
Denver, CO 80239
303-371-6550

Wood-Mode Cabinetry
Wood Metal Industries
One Second Street
Kreamer, PA 17833
717-374-2711

COUNTERTOPS

American Olean Tile Co., Inc.
PO Box 271
Lansdale, PA 19446
215-855-1111

Avonite, Inc.
5100 Goldleaf Circle
Suite 200
Los Angeles, CA 90056
800-4-AVONITE
800-428-6648 (Calif)

Color Tile
See listing for FLOORING

Corian Building Products
E. I. DuPont de Nemours
& Co.
1007 Market Street
Wilmington, DE 19898
800-441-7515

Dal-Tile
See listing for FLOORING

Formica Corp.
One Stanford Road
PO Box 338
Piscataway, NJ 08854
201-469-1555

Nevamar Corp.
8339 Telegraph Road
Odenton, MD 21113
301-551-5000

Summitville Tiles, Inc.
Summitville, OH 43962
216-223-1511

Wilsonart
Ralph Wilson Plastics Co.
600 General Bruce Drive
Temple, TX 76501
800-433-3222
800-792-6000 (Texas)

FLOORING

American Olean Tile Co., Inc.
PO Box 271
Lansdale, PA 19446
215-855-1111

Armstrong World Industries, Inc.
PO Box 3001
Lancaster, PA 17604
800-233-3823

Bruce Hardwood Floors
PO Box 660100
Dallas, TX 75266-0100
214-931-3000

Color Tile
PO Box 2475
Fort Worth, TX 76113
817-870-9400

Congoleum Corp.
861 Sloan Avenue
Trenton, NJ 08619
609-584-3000

Dal-Tile
7834 Hawn Freeway
Dallas, TX 75217
214-398-1411

Mannington Mills, Inc.
PO Box 30
Salem, NJ 08079
609-935-3000

Summitville Tiles, Inc.
Summitville, OH 43962
216-223-1511

LIGHT FIXTURES

Casablanca Fan Co.
PO Box 424
City of Industry, CA 91747
818-369-6441

Halo Lighting
6842 Walker Street
La Palma, CA 90623
714-522-7171

Hunter Fan Co.
2500 Frisco Avenue
Memphis, TN 38114
901-743-1360

Lightolier/Genlyte
100 Lighting Way
Secaucus, NJ 07096-1508
201-864-3000

Progress Lighting
Erie Avenue & G Street
Philadelphia, PA 19134
215-289-1200

SINKS & FITTINGS

ABBAKA
435 23rd Street
San Francisco, CA 94107
415-648-7210

American Standard, Inc.
U.S. Plumbing Products
PO Box 6820
Piscataway, NJ 08855
201-980-3000

Blanco Sinks
Western States Manufac-
turing Corp.
1559 Sunland Lane
Costa Mesa, CA 92626
714-557-1933

The Chicago Faucet Co.
2100 S. Nuclear Drive
Des Plaines, IL 60018
312-694-4400

Culligan International Co.
One Culligan Parkway
Northbrook, IL 60062
708-205-6000

Delta Faucet Co.
55 E. 11th Street
PO Box 40980
Indianapolis, IN 46280
317-848-1812

Eljer
PO Box 869037
Plano, TX 75086-9037
214-881-7177

Elkay Manufacturing
2222 Camden Court
Oak Brook, IL 60521
708-574-8484

Everpure Filtration Systems
660 N. Blackhawk Drive
Westmont, IL 60559
312-654-4000

Franke, Inc.
Kitchen Systems Division
Box 428
Hatfield, PA 19440
800-626-5771

Grohe America, Inc.
900 Lively Boulevard
Wood Dale, IL 60191
708-350-2600

In-Sink-Erator Division
Emerson Electric Co.
4700 21st Street
Racine, WI 53406
800-558-5712

Jenn-Air Co.
3035 Shadeland
Indianapolis, IN 46226
317-545-2271

KitchenAid Inc.
701 Main Street
St. Joseph, MI 49085
616-982-4500

Kohler Co.
444 Highland Drive
Kohler, WI 53044
414-457-4441

KWC Faucets
Western States Manufac-
turing Corp.
1559 Sunland Lane
Costa Mesa, CA 92626
714-557-1933

Luwa Corp.
PO Box 16348
Charlotte, NC 28297
704-394-8341

Porcher Sinks
650 Maple Avenue
Torrance, CA 90503
213-212-6112

STORAGE PRODUCTS

Closet Maid
Clairson International
720 SW 17th Street
Ocala, FL 32674
904-351-6100

Elfa/Eurica Marketing, Inc.
1760 East Wilshire Avenue
Santa Ana, CA 92705-4615
714-285-1000

Iron-A-Way, Inc.
220 W. Jackson
Morton, IL 61550
309-266-7232

Rev-a-Shelf, Inc.
2409 Plantside Drive
PO Box 99585
Jefferson, KY 40299
800-626-1126
502-499-5835

Rubbermaid Inc.
1147 Akron Rd.
Wooster, OH 44691
216-264-6464

INDEX